Praise for *Q# Pocket Guide*

A no-nonsense, comprehensive guide for physicists and programmers to get started with Q#. A succinct, yet thorough approach that covers both mastering the basics and accessing libraries for more specialist applications.

—*Nicholas Harrigan, author of*
Programming Quantum Computers

This helpful and practical guide will increase creativity and productivity in your day-to-day quantum computing.

—*Mathias Soeken,*
Quantum Software Engineer, Microsoft

Q# Pocket Guide
Instant Help for Q# Developers

Mariia Mykhailova

Beijing · Boston · Farnham · Sebastopol · Tokyo

Q# Pocket Guide

by Mariia Mykhailova

Published by O'Reilly Media, Inc., 1005 Gravenstein Highway North, Sebastopol, CA 95472.

O'Reilly books may be purchased for educational, business, or sales promotional use. Online editions are also available for most titles (*http://oreilly.com*). For more information, contact our corporate/institutional sales department: 800-998-9938 or *corporate@oreilly.com*.

Acquisitions Editor: Suzanne McQuade
Development Editor: Sarah Grey
Production Editor: Elizabeth Faerm
Copyeditor: Piper Editorial Consulting, LLC
Proofreader: Arthur Johnson
Indexer: Ellen Troutman-Zaig
Interior Designer: David Futato
Cover Designer: Karen Montgomery
Illustrator: Kate Dullea

June 2022:   First Edition

Revision History for the First Edition
    2022-06-14:   First Release

See *https://oreil.ly/qpgERR* for release details.

978-1-098-10886-1

[LSI]

Table of Contents

Part II.   Using the Microsoft Quantum Development Kit

Foreword

When I first learned in the late '90s of a different model of computation, I was instantly inspired and intrigued. How could there be another way for a computer to compute? How would that machine perform operations? What would it mean to program such a machine? My fascination led to my two-decade exploration of answers to such questions, an exploration that now is witness to a growing community of quantum developers, engineers, researchers, and enthusiasts, and an industry working to realize quantum advantage, the demonstration of an algorithm running on a quantum computer that gives a solution more powerful or faster than the best-known classical solution.

But the real impact comes when quantum advantage is *practical*—when we have solutions for *practical* problems of real-world interest, and those solutions have *practical* runtimes of less than a few weeks.

Practical is essential. As a computer scientist, I see the magic of quantum computers through the lens of a language, and through the ability to program, form a recipe, and efficiently express what we need the machine to do. The underlying instructions, operations, and programming model of a quantum computer are just different, and we need a different way to program it—a practical way that artfully captures the interplay between the highly hybrid nature of quantum algorithms and their quantum and classical needs.

And practicality is what comes to mind in reading Mariia's new book. Over the last five years, Mariia, along with a broader team of quantum software engineers and researchers, has been building out a new way to express programs for a quantum computer, and working to make it easier to bring quantum mechanical properties to life through simple, expressive language and examples.

We know that improvements in hardware performance can drive changes in what's possible, and so too can changes in algorithms. An entire industry is working to scale up quantum machines, with a focus on improving the quantum chip and devices. But to achieve quantum advantage, and to chip away at even more advances and areas in which quantum computers will make a difference, we need more algorithms, and we need more practical algorithms.

With the introduction of Fortran, algorithm designers became more efficient—by using a more practical language for their needs, they were able to express algorithms and programs faster. They were able to bring their intuition to their code. They were readily able to explore the vast set of opportunities for a classical machine.

We need a similar capability in quantum computing. The Q# programming language has been designed to enable algorithm development, not just low-level instruction programs, and aims to empower the programmer to think about the algorithm design rather than the details of the physics.

With this pocket guide, Mariia brings to life her own experience in quantum development with Q#, weaving her expert perspectives and insights into simple, easy-to-use definitions, examples, and debugging tools. Mariia showcases the nuances of quantum programming, the unique features of Q# that enable more extensive algorithm development, and how to use advanced features of the language to bring your program to "quantum" life.

I hope this guide enables you to join the exploration for more quantum applications and helps seed a generation of quantum developers and algorithm designers. Developing practical quantum advantage requires our collective intelligence and a growing community of quantum programmers. Quantum programming must be practical for the scale of development needed to happen. And this guide is your next step toward quantum practicality. You never know—you may just invent the next groundbreaking quantum application.

—*Dr. Krysta M. Svore*
Distinguished Engineer, VP
Quantum Software, Microsoft
May 2022

Preface

Quantum computing is a fascinating computing paradigm, and reasoning about it requires different languages than for classical computing. One of the ways to think about quantum computing is quantum programming, which takes familiar software engineering tools and adapts them to express quantum concepts and implement and evaluate algorithms. Quantum programming is a much younger discipline than either quantum computing or classical programming, yet multiple quantum programming languages and software toolkits have already emerged to help software engineers and researchers.

Q# is a domain-specific quantum programming language created to express quantum algorithms. It is part of the Microsoft Quantum Development Kit (QDK), a set of tools to support quantum software engineering. Both Q# and the QDK are designed for working with high-level algorithms rather than low-level ones ("circuits") and include a variety of language features, libraries, and developer tools to support that goal.

This book offers all the information you'll need to start developing and running Q# applications, including complete code examples and discussions of the tools available for every step of the quantum software development cycle.

Why I Wrote This Book

I joined Microsoft Quantum in early 2017, just in time to witness the inception of the programming language that was later named Q#, and to participate in the development of the first release of the QDK. Over time I've gravitated toward education and outreach work, helping people learn quantum computing and quantum programming using our tools—and making it interesting.

This book is the summary of my experience with Q#, both using it myself and helping others figure out its more useful—or more obscure!—language features. It is by no means an exhaustive treatise, but I hope that this book will lead you to appreciate Q# and use it more effectively, and inspire you to dive deeper in its ecosystem.

Who This Book Is For

If you want to build quantum computing applications using Q# and the QDK, this book is for you! The book combines a thorough coverage of the basics with detailed code examples and deep dives into quantum-specific language features, so you'll find something new and interesting whether you're completely new to Q# or you have experience with it already.

However, this book is *not* an introduction to quantum computing! Throughout the book I assume that you're already familiar with the basic concepts of quantum computing, such as qubits, quantum gates, and measurements.

If you're looking to get started with both quantum computing and quantum programming at the same time, I recommend you combine this book with any resource that covers the basic concepts of quantum computing, such as the Quantum Katas (*https://oreil.ly/w19qn*), a collection of tutorials and programming exercises on quantum computing. This way you'll be able to learn new topics and immediately put them to good use solving problems and implementing the solutions. After all, the best way to learn is by doing!

Navigating This Book

This book consists of two parts. Part I details the Q# programming language, including its syntax and constructs, and shows you how to write Q# code.

- Chapter 1 gives a high-level overview of Q# program structure and introduces the main elements of Q# code: namespaces, operations and functions, user-defined type definitions, and comments.

- Chapter 2 covers the data types offered by Q#, from primitive data types (both classical and quantum) to data structures such as arrays and tuples, and offers a deeper dive into user-defined types. I pay special attention to the way Q# represents qubits, since this data type is fundamentally different from anything you've encountered in programming languages for classical computing.

- Chapter 3 covers the expressions and operators available in Q#. Most Q# expressions have equivalents in classical programming languages, though sometimes they feature different syntax, and only a few are uniquely quantum, so this chapter is relatively brief.

- Chapter 4 describes the statements supported by Q#. As in Chapter 3, Q#'s classical statements are likely familiar to you from other programming languages, and only several statements are specific to quantum programs, most prominently the qubit allocation statement.

- Chapter 5 dives deeper into operations and functions in Q#—the subroutines that make up most of Q# code. This is the most dense chapter in Part I, since it has to cover a lot of ground, from the basic syntax of defining a callable to more advanced topics such as the functional elements of Q# and defining type-parameterized callables.

I also spend a lot of time on the quantum-specific topics, such as representing quantum gates and measurements, as well as neat capabilities such as generating adjoint and controlled specializations of gates automatically and using these specializations.

Part II gives an overview of the quantum software development lifecycle and the tools offered by the QDK for its various stages, helping you put your Q# code into practice.

- Chapter 6 introduces quantum software development and simulators—classical programs that allow you to simulate various aspects of quantum systems and thus to execute and evaluate quantum programs without access to quantum hardware. After this, the chapter delves into the various ways to run Q# programs, whether on their own or interwoven with classical programs, and in different environments.

- Chapter 7 is an overview of the Q# libraries shipped as part of the QDK. These help you keep your Q# programs readable and focus on the high-level logic rather than on circuit-level implementation.

- Finally, Chapter 8 describes the variety of tools and techniques available to the Q# developer for inspecting and visualizing various elements of their programs, testing them, and debugging them.

Conventions Used in This Book

The following typographical conventions are used in this book:

Italic

Indicates new terms, URLs, email addresses, filenames, and file extensions.

`Constant width`

> Used for program listings, as well as within paragraphs to refer to program elements such as variable or function names, databases, data types, environment variables, statements, and keywords.

`Constant width bold`

> Shows commands or other text that should be typed literally by the user.

`Constant width italic`

> Shows text that should be replaced with user-supplied values or by values determined by context.

NOTE

This element signifies a general note.

Using Code Examples

Supplemental material (code examples, exercises, etc.) is available for download at *https://github.com/tcNickolas/q-sharp-pocket-guide-samples*.

If you have a technical question or a problem using the code examples, please send email to *bookquestions@oreilly.com*.

This book is here to help you get your job done. In general, if example code is offered with this book, you may use it in your programs and documentation. You do not need to contact us for permission unless you're reproducing a significant portion of the code. For example, writing a program that uses several chunks of code from this book does not require permission. Selling or distributing examples from O'Reilly books does require permission. Answering a question by citing this book and quoting example code does not require permission. Incorporating a significant amount of example code from this book into your product's documentation does require permission.

We appreciate, but generally do not require, attribution. An attribution usually includes the title, author, publisher, and ISBN. For example: "*Q# Pocket Guide* by Mariia Mykhailova (O'Reilly). Copyright 2022 Mariia Mykhailova, 978-1-098-10886-1."

If you feel your use of code examples falls outside fair use or outside the permission given above, feel free to contact us at *permissions@oreilly.com*.

O'Reilly Online Learning

 For more than 40 years, *O'Reilly Media* has provided technology and business training, knowledge, and insight to help companies succeed.

Our unique network of experts and innovators share their knowledge and expertise through books, articles, and our online learning platform. O'Reilly's online learning platform gives you on-demand access to live training courses, in-depth learning paths, interactive coding environments, and a vast collection of text and video from O'Reilly and 200+ other publishers. For more information, visit *http://oreilly.com*.

How to Contact Us

Please address comments and questions concerning this book to the publisher:

O'Reilly Media, Inc.
1005 Gravenstein Highway North
Sebastopol, CA 95472
800-998-9938 (in the United States or Canada)
707-829-0515 (international or local)
707-829-0104 (fax)

We have a web page for this book, where we list errata, examples, and any additional information. You can access this page at *https://oreil.ly/q-sharp-pocket-guide*.

Email *bookquestions@oreilly.com* to comment or ask technical questions about this book.

For news and information about our books and courses, visit *https://oreilly.com*.

Find us on LinkedIn: *https://linkedin.com/company/oreilly-media*.

Follow us on Twitter: *https://twitter.com/oreillymedia*.

Watch us on YouTube: *https://youtube.com/oreillymedia*.

Acknowledgments

I am grateful to my wonderful editors, Suzanne McQuade, Sarah Grey, and Elizabeth Faerm, and the rest of the great team at O'Reilly who worked to make this book a reality.

I would like to thank my reviewers, Mathias Soeken, Nicholas Harrigan, Alan Geller, and Tony Holdroyd, for their technical insight and attention to detail, and Krysta Svore for writing the foreword for the book. Eric Johnston deserves a special mention for introducing me to Suzanne—without him this book wouldn't have happened!

Finally, I am infinitely grateful to my beloved husband, Sergii Dymchenko, my friends, and everybody who supported me and cheered me on throughout the year I spent writing this book.

Q# Programming Language

CHAPTER 1

Program Structure

This chapter offers an overview of Q# program structure and the main elements it comprises. This will help you orient yourself in the following chapters, in which we'll dive deeper into writing Q# code.

Your First Q# Program

Example 1-1 shows a Q# program that prints a message to the console. While very simple, it shows the main elements of Q# code: a namespace, an open directive, an operation that contains the actual Q# statements, and comments.

NOTE

The code samples in Part I of this book are written as Q# standalone applications. You can follow the installation instructions (*https://oreil.ly/cKJZz*) to set up the Microsoft Quantum Development Kit for your environment and run these samples. In Chapter 6, we'll discuss different ways to run Q# programs and the nuances of writing Q# code for each of them.

Example 1-1. "Hello World" program in Q#

```
namespace HelloQuantumWorld {
    open Microsoft.Quantum.Intrinsic; // To use Message

    /// # Summary
    /// Prints a message to the console.
    @EntryPoint()
    operation SayHello() : Unit {
        Message("Hello quantum world!");
    }
}
```

NOTE

Once you've installed the QDK for your preferred development environment, you can create a Q# project, copy-paste
Example 1-1 to the *.qs* file in the project, and run it following these instructions (*https://oreil.ly/Uup9d*). You should
see a console window with this text message in it:

```
Hello quantum world!
```

Congratulations, you just ran your first Q# program!

Let's take a closer look at the code elements that are shown in
Example 1-1.

Namespaces

At the outermost level, all Q# code is organized into namespaces. A *namespace* is a collection of uniquely named operations,
functions (collectively referred to as *callables*), and user-defined
types.

The `namespace` keyword defines a namespace for the Q# code
within the following block:

```
namespace HelloQuantumWorld {
    // Operations, functions, and user-defined
```

```
    // types within this block will belong to
    // the namespace HelloQuantumWorld.
}
```

The namespace name can contain letters, digits, underscores, and dots.

Unlike .NET languages, Q# doesn't have a hierarchy of nested namespaces defined by the dots in their names. Namespaces cannot be nested inside each other. Namespaces with names that contain each other can be related logically, but this relation will not be reflected on the code level.

For example, Q# libraries offer the logically connected namespaces `Microsoft.Quantum.MachineLearning` and `Microsoft.Quantum.MachineLearning.Datasets`, but the operations defined in the latter are defined independently from the former.

All Q# code, except comments, must be included in a namespace. (Q# code snippets written in Jupyter Notebooks may seem to be an exception from this rule, as they cannot be defined inside a namespace. However, internally, Jupyter Notebooks paste the contents of Q# code cells into a temporary namespace before compiling them. We will discuss the nuances of writing Q# code in Jupyter Notebooks in more detail in Chapter 6.)

The code within a namespace can access any other code declared in the same namespace without extra qualification. To access a callable or a user-defined type declared in a different namespace, you have to use either its fully qualified name or an open directive.

A *fully qualified name* of a callable or a type is its namespace name, followed by a dot and its unqualified name:

```
// This uses the fully qualified operation name.
Microsoft.Quantum.Intrinsic.Message("Hello!");
```

An *open directive* imports all callables and types from that namespace and makes them available as if they were defined in the current namespace. Open directives must be the first element within the namespace:

```
// Open the namespace which defines Message.
open Microsoft.Quantum.Intrinsic;

// Use unqualified name of the operation.
Message("Hello!");
```

Note that a callable definition in the current namespace has precedence over any definitions of callables with the same name in other open namespaces. Two callables with the same name coming from different open namespaces, other than the current namespace, don't have precedence over each other, so you have to use the fully qualified name to specify which one you want to call.

Open directives also allow you to define *namespace aliases*, which you can use instead of full namespace names when qualifying callables or types from those namespaces. This can be useful, for example, to disambiguate if operations with the same name are defined in two open namespaces. Defining an alias for a namespace doesn't open it:

```
// Create an alias for the namespace which
// defines Message (without opening it).
open Microsoft.Quantum.Intrinsic as Builtin;

// Use the alias with the operation name.
Builtin.Message("Hello!");
```

Operations and Functions

The main element of namespaces that holds most of the Q# code is operations and functions—series of statements that perform certain actions. *Operations* are general-purpose *subroutines*—sequences of instructions that perform a certain task, packaged as a unit. *Functions* are a special type of subroutines that perform only deterministic classical computations. By contrast, operations have no restrictions on the actions they perform, and they may or may not involve quantum computations.

An operation declaration will use the keyword operation, followed by the operation name, the list of its input parameters, and the type of its return:

```
operation SayHello() : Unit {
    Message("Hello quantum world!");
}
```

In this example, we define an operation called SayHello, which takes no parameters and has no return, as denoted by the Unit return type. (I'll talk more about the uses of Unit in Chapter 2.) The only thing it does is print the message to the console.

Including the @EntryPoint() attribute before the operation SayHello marks the operation that will be called first when the Q# standalone application is executed (more on that in Chapter 6).

Functions are defined similarly, using the keyword function instead of operation.

Operations and functions are a fundamental concept in Q#, and there is a lot more to defining them than has been mentioned here. We will discuss defining operations and functions in more detail in Chapter 5. Meanwhile, this summary should help you read the basic code samples in the following chapters.

Type Declarations

Another namespace element is *type declarations*—declarations of user-defined types. *User-defined types* are tuples of named and anonymous items of other types (primitive or user-defined).

The newtype keyword declares a user-defined type:

```
// Declare type for pair.
newtype Pair = (First : Int, Second : Int);
```

We will discuss declaring user-defined types in more detail in Chapter 2.

Comments

Q# offers two types of comments—implementation comments (more often referred to as single-line comments) and documentation comments.

Implementation comments allow you to include notes on the Q# code in the code itself. They are intended for other developers working on the same code—your teammates or even your future self—and should offer additional context that might not be clear from the code itself: the design decisions made during code development, links to resources describing the techniques used, etc.

A single-line comment begins with two forward slashes (`//`) and ends at the end of the line:

```
// This is a single-line comment.
let a = 1;    // Can start mid-line.
```

Q# doesn't currently support multiline (block) comments.

Documentation comments allow you to embed the external documentation for your Q# code into the code itself. Their audience is the users of your code, and they should describe the purpose of the code and the meaning and the format of the input parameters, offer usage examples, and so forth.

A documentation comment begins with three forward slashes (`///`) and ends at the end of the line. Documentation comments appear in blocks preceding operations, functions, or type declarations:

```
/// # Summary
/// Prints a message to the console.
operation SayHello() : Unit {
    Message("Hello quantum world!");
}
```

The Q# compiler parses documentation comments to provide quick info in IDEs that offer IntelliSense support for Q#, such as Visual Studio and Visual Studio Code. Figure 1-1 shows an example of the quick info window in VS Code.

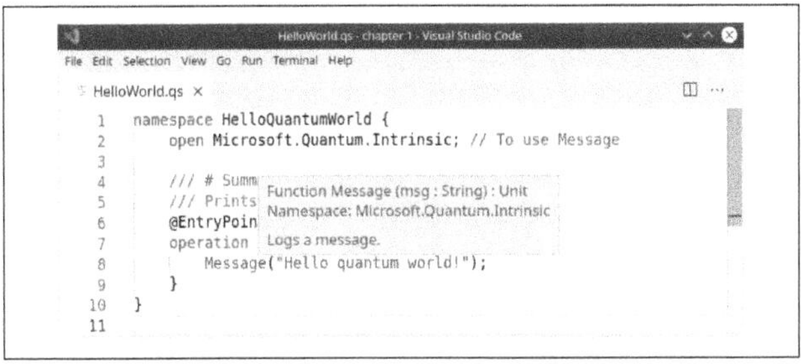

Figure 1-1. Quick info window in Visual Studio Code

Additionally, the Q# documentation generator uses documentation comments in Q# libraries' source code to generate the API reference (*https://oreil.ly/GvpHK*).

You can use Markdown language (*https://oreil.ly/SVsIM*) in the documentation comments you write to enable formatting and cross-references in the generated API documentation, and LaTeX (*https://oreil.ly/371Q4*) to support math formulas. The Q# documentation page on comments (*https://oreil.ly/P4nUq*) provides more information on the structure of documentation comments.

Conclusion

Now that you're familiar with the high-level structure of Q# programs and running them, you are ready to dive deeper into the Q# programming language. In the next chapter, you will learn about the data types offered by Q# and learn to create your own user-defined types.

CHAPTER 2

Data Types

This chapter offers an overview of the Q# type system: the data types available in Q# and the corresponding literals.

The chapter starts with a review of the Q# type system and the principles it follows. Then I cover *primitive data types*—classical, which have equivalents in classical programming languages, and quantum, which are specific to quantum programs. After that I introduce *data structures*—arrays, tuples, and user-defined types. Note that in this chapter I'll focus on the data types themselves, and I'll cover the operators and expressions used to work with values of each type in Chapter 3.

Q# supports elements of functional programming, which means it treats operations and functions similarly to other data types. However, this topic deserves special attention, so I'll discuss Q# operations and functions separately in Chapter 5.

The Q# Type System

Let's start with a quick review of Q#'s *type system*: the set of rules and principles that assign types to various elements of a program, such as variables, expressions, or callables. The following principles will give you a good idea of how Q# types work.

Q# is a type-safe language.

Q# doesn't allow operations or type conversions that violate the rules of the type system.

Q# is statically typed.

All type checking is done during compile time, rather than during the program execution. The types are associated with variables, similar to C#, rather than with values, as in Python: once the Q# compiler determines that a variable has a certain type, then attempting to assign a value of different type to it will cause a compilation error. This allows the compiler to detect errors in rarely used code paths, and to make compiled programs more efficient.

Q# uses a mix of implicit and explicit type declarations.

Q# doesn't support explicit type declarations of variables, like the ones you would see in C++ or Java. Instead, it uses Hindley–Milner *type inference* (*https://oreil.ly/Pu8PY*) to deduce the type of the variable automatically by evaluating the type of the expression assigned to it or the later uses of the variable. However, when defining an operation or a function, you have to declare the types of its parameters and its return value explicitly.

Q# is strongly typed.

Q# restricts intermixing operations on different data types. For example, it prohibits implicit type conversions, unlike a lot of classical languages such as C++ or Python. If you want to use an `Int` value in a context that expects a `Double` type, you have to use the library function `IntAsDouble` to perform an explicit type cast.

Q# is nominally typed.

Q# determines compatibility of data types using their names; two types with identical structure but different names are different. This is most important when working with user-defined types. For example, library types `BigEndian` and `LittleEndian` are effectively both arrays of qubits, but you cannot pass a `BigEndian` value or a qubit

---

array when a `LittleEndian` is expected without using a library function to perform an explicit cast.

Q# types are value types.

Q# doesn't support references or pointers, unlike a lot of classical languages such as C# or Java. All Q# types are value types: they store their data directly, rather than storing pointers to their data like reference types do. When you change the value of a mutable variable (I'll discuss mutable variables in Chapter 4), Q# doesn't mutate that value itself; instead, it creates a new value and assigns it to the variable. For example, consider the following code that defines two arrays:

```
let a = [1, 2, 3];
mutable b = a;
set a w/= 0 <- 0;    // Now a is [0, 2, 3]
set b w/= 2 <- 4;    // Now b is [1, 2, 4]
```

Assigning array a to array b creates a copy of the value stored in a at the time of assignment and stores it in b. After that, updating one of the arrays is completely independent from the other one. Contrast this with C#, in which arrays are reference types, and similar code produces two array variables pointing to the same value [0, 2, 4].

NOTE

The Q# code snippets in this chapter and in Chapter 3 illustrate the behavior of data types and expressions using variable definitions. We'll discuss handling variables in detail in Chapter 4, but understanding the main statements will make the code examples easier to read until then. The `let` and `mutable` statements are used to declare immutable and mutable variables, respectively, and the `set` statement is used to reassign mutable variables. In particular, the `set` statements in this code snippet are used to replace one element of the array.

Q# supports elements of functional programming.

Q# considers operations and functions to be *first-class citizens*: it treats them similarly to other data types, which means that you can assign them to variables, pass them as parameters, and return them from other operations and functions. This allows you to write elegant generic programs and libraries, such as implementations of algorithms that use quantum oracles (see Chapter 5).

Now that you're familiar with the principles on which the Q# type system is built, let's take a closer look at the data types it supports, starting with the simplest ones.

Primitive Classical Data Types

Q# supports a number of primitive data types that mirror the primitive types found in most classical programming languages. Their behavior is very close to that of their counterparts in other languages, so I won't go into too much detail.

Unit

A type with a single possible value, the literal (). This type is most frequently used to indicate that an operation doesn't have a return value, similar to the void type in C++. It can also be used as an operation parameter, though scenarios in which it is helpful are very rare.

Int

A 64-bit signed integer. The values range from -2^{63} = -9,223,372,036,854,775,808 to 2^{63} - 1 = 9,223,372,036,854,775,807. Int literals can be written in Q# code in decimal (no prefix), binary (prefix 0b), octal (prefix 0o), and hexadecimal (prefix 0x) representations.

BigInt

A signed integer of arbitrary size. BigInt literals are written similarly to Int literals, but with an L postfix: 0L is a BigInt literal, while 0 is an Int literal.

Double

A 64-bit floating-point number. The values range from -1.7976931348623157E+308 to 1.7976931348623157E+308. NaN ("not a number") is a valid Double literal, similar to .NET languages, but Infinity and NegativeInfinity are not; they can be obtained only as a result of arithmetic operation.

Bool

A Boolean value. The values are true and false.

String

A string of UTF-16 characters and code units. String literals are sequences of Unicode characters enclosed in double quotation marks ("). Q# strings use backslash (\) to escape special characters such as double quotation marks (\"), newline (\n), and tab (\t).

Q# also supports *interpolated strings*—string literals that start with $ before the opening double quotation mark and contain interpolation expressions enclosed in curly brackets. When an interpolated string is resolved, the interpolation expressions are replaced with the results of their evaluation, converted to strings. For example, an interpolated string $"Hello, {readerName}!" will resolve to a greeting to the reader using the name they defined in the readerName variable earlier in the program.

Range

A sequence of integers that represents an arithmetic progression, that is, a sequence with constant difference between consecutive terms. Range literals are expressions of the form start..step..stop, where start, step, and stop are literals or expressions of type Int. start is the first element of the sequence, step is the difference between consecutive terms, and stop is the "exit criteria" for the range generator: the range includes numbers start, start + step, and so on, until the value stop is passed. The ranges are inclusive, i.e., if stop - start is divisible by `step`, `stop` will be included in the range. Range steps can be positive or negative, but not 0. Q# programs frequently use ranges with step size 1 (for example, with `for` loops, as we'll discuss in Chapter 4); in such cases, you can omit the step parameter and define the range as `start..stop`. A range can be empty if the step is positive and `start > stop`, or if the step is negative and `start < stop`.

As I've mentioned before, Q# doesn't support implicit type conversion between types, whether they are primitive or more complicated. If you need to convert one type to another, you'll need to do type conversion explicitly. For example, you'll use library functions such as `IntAsDouble` or `IntAsBigInt` to convert between types if you need to multiply two numbers of different types (see Chapter 7), or a conditional expression if you need to convert a Boolean to an integer (see Chapter 3).

Qubits

Since Q# is a quantum programming language, it supports several data types that are unique to quantum computing and do not have an equivalent in classical programming languages. The most fundamental of the quantum data types is the `Qubit`, which represents qubits used by a quantum program.

The Q# language treats qubits differently from classical data types, which are passive memory units that store information without processing it. Instead, qubits are *execution units*—parts of a quantum processing unit that perform the computations following the instructions of the quantum program (the gates and the measurements applied to them).

Physics-Imposed Constraints

Q# is designed to write programs that run on quantum hardware, so it doesn't support nonphysical operations—that is, operations that would violate the rules of quantum physics.

Operations such as explicitly setting the qubits to a certain state or directly inspecting their state would violate the laws of physics, so you can't perform them in Q# code. In fact, Q# does not allow you to interact directly with the quantum state of your program, and the quantum state of the program is not reflected in Q# on the language level.

For example, you can't assign a certain state to the qubits your program uses or access information about the program's quantum state beyond what doing a measurement tells you. Contrast this with the mathematical notation used to describe quantum algorithms in theoretical discussions, in which you always spell out the quantum state of the system after each step, either as a vector of complex numbers or as a sum of basis states in Dirac notation, giving the illusion that the state is transparent and accessible.

Instead, you need to come up with a "physical" way to do these operations the way you would do them on a quantum device. For example, if you need qubits in a certain state, you need to allocate them in the $|0\rangle$ state and transform them to the required state by applying the right sequence of gates. Q# libraries offer some routines to help you prepare quantum states; see Chapter 7 for details.

Similarly, quantum physics doesn't allow you to inspect detailed information about the quantum state of the system, so Q# doesn't allow you to do it programmatically—at least not when running a program on quantum hardware. To facilitate quantum software development, Q# offers tools that allow you to inspect the system state—but only if the program is running on a quantum simulator instead of an actual quantum device. I'll talk more about quantum simulators in Chapter 6, and I'll show you the tools that are available for program inspection in Chapter 8.

Abstracting Away Physical Implementation

While the logic of handling qubits in Q# follows the general rules of quantum physics, Q# doesn't express the details of qubits' physical realization on the language level. Qubits in Q# programs are abstract units of quantum computation that the program uses to express the logic of the quantum algorithm it implements. In contrast, the qubits you can find in a quantum device are *physical qubits*: particles or physical devices that behave as two-level quantum systems, allowing the quantum device to carry out computations.

Current quantum hardware relies on physical qubits with high error rates and low coherence times, making it impossible to use them to carry out long computations. In addition, different hardware platforms use different technologies for implementing physical qubits and impose different limitations on the operations you can perform with them.

This means that developing programs that control physical qubits directly is actually a lot like coding in an assembly language (*https://oreil.ly/Oa6CF*): it is low level, platform specific, and not easily portable between technologies or even between different implementations of the same technology.

In contrast, Q# is a high-level quantum programming language: it allows you to develop your application in terms of the logic of the computation you need to perform, without worrying about the physical reality of the qubits your program will run on. Under the hood, the Q# compiler and runtime will take care of everything needed to run your program on a specific simulator or hardware device. This can include multiple transformations of your program, such as:

- Performing *error correction*, which includes encoding each logical qubit allocated by the program using multiple physical qubits and translating the logical operations performed on the logical qubits into sequences of operations on physical qubits

---

- Performing *gate synthesis*, or translating the logical gates that need to be applied to the qubits into the corresponding sequences of gates natively implemented by the physical device

- Translating the gates that need to be applied to qubits into control pulses and sending them to the devices that implement these qubits

The Qubit Data Type

Since the Qubit data type has to match the physical reality of quantum systems, the language handles it quite differently from other data types. Let's look at a few such differences.

Qubit is an *opaque data type*—a data type whose structure is not defined in its interface. Qubits have an internal state that you cannot access or modify directly. Instead, you can change the quantum state of the program using quantum gates and extract some information about it using quantum measurements (potentially changing the state in the process).

There are no literals of the Qubit data type. Q# programs *allocate* and *release* qubits instead of creating new variables and assigning Qubit literals to them.

Classical host code cannot pass a Qubit data type to Q# code as a parameter or receive it as a return value. The Q# compiler requires full information about the quantum program, including all qubit allocations and releases, to be able to analyze and optimize the code. A Q# program always starts with no qubits allocated, and the only qubits it uses are the ones it allocates itself.

Finally, copying variables of type Qubit copies references to them instead of values. Consider the following code snippet:

```
use a = Qubit();
let b = a;
```

At a glance this code seems to violate the no-cloning theorem: qubit b is a copy of qubit a! However, copying qubit a doesn't actually allocate a new qubit with a state that is a copy of the original qubit state. Instead, variables a and b both contain pointers to the same allocated qubit; the pointer is copied, but the underlying qubit object remains the same. This is different from copying other data types, such as arrays, in which Q# creates another instance of the value being copied.

Other Primitive Quantum Data Types

The other two primitive quantum data types are a lot less sophisticated, though they are useful for expressing quantum programs.

Measurement Results

Result data type represents a measurement result. The values are Zero (which corresponds to the eigenvalue +1) and One (eigenvalue –1). Q# defines a separate data type for representing measurement results instead of reusing Int or Bool to emphasize its domain-specific meaning and behavior. Indeed, measurement results do not naturally support arithmetic or logical operations on them, like integers and Booleans do. Instead, if your specific algorithm requires performing computations based on measurement results, you can convert a measurement result to a different data type using library functions such as ResultAsBool or ResultArrayAsInt.

Pauli Matrices

Pauli data type represents a single-qubit Pauli matrix (*https:// oreil.ly/YTUw8*)—one of the four 2×2 matrices that describe common single-qubit quantum gates and together form a basis in the space of all single-qubit quantum gates. The values are PauliI, PauliX, PauliY, or PauliZ. This data type is typically used to define measurements in a basis different from the computational basis, for both single-qubit and multiqubit measurements.

Representing Quantum Gates and Measurements

Earlier in this chapter, I mentioned that some common quantum computing concepts don't have a primitive data type defined to represent them, the quantum states being the most prominent example. Furthermore, quantum gates and quantum measurements are not built-in data types either! Instead, they are implemented as operations acting on qubits, which return data type Unit (gates) or Result (measurements). This allows Q# to treat the built-in ("intrinsic") gates and measurements in the same way as more complex user-defined operations. I will discuss the operations in more detail in Chapter 5, and the set of built-in gates and measurements in Chapter 7.

Now that you're familiar with all primitive types supported by Q#, let's dive into the next class of data types: data structures.

Data Structures

Q# supports three kinds of data structures: arrays, tuples, and user-defined types. Since Q# is a domain-specific language, it doesn't need a rich system of data structures like general-purpose languages do.

Arrays

An *array* is a sequence of values of the same type. The underlying type of the sequence elements can be any type from the Q# type system: a primitive type, a data structure, or a callable. The type of an array of type T is written as T[].

Q# offers several types of array literals to define general arrays, empty arrays, and arrays of repeated elements.

A *general array literal* is a comma-separated sequence of one or more expressions, enclosed in square brackets: [expr1, expr2, ..., exprN]. The expressions must be of the same type or (in the case of operations) have a common base type; the array will be an array of that type. For example, to define an array of floating-point numbers, you need to cast all elements of it to Double explicitly.

The *empty array literal* is just a pair of square brackets: []. Note that this literal doesn't specify the type of the array it creates. Instead, its type will be inferred later based on how you use the array variable, such as passing it as an argument to a callable or appending elements to it. If the type of the array cannot be inferred based on its later use, you cannot use this literal.

Finally, a *repeated constant array literal* is an array element expression, followed by a comma, a size = keyword, and the length of the array, enclosed in square brackets: [elementExpr, size = N]. The expression that defines the value of the array element is reevaluated for each element; for example, [Draw RandomBool(0.5), size = 10] will produce an array of independent random values, rather than picking a single value randomly and replicating it.

Deprecated Array Literal: new Expression

Prior to version 0.16, Q# supported only one way to define an array literal, besides explicitly specifying all array elements: the new expression. The expression new T[N] creates an array of type T of length N, filled with *default values* of type T. Default values of types are used only in the context of array creation; Table 2-1 lists the default values for various types.

Table 2-1. Default values for Q# data types

Data type(s)	Default value
Int, BigInt, Double	Zero of the corresponding type
Bool	false
String	""

Data type(s)	Default value
Result	Zero
Pauli	PauliI
Range	empty range
Array	array of length 0

However, not all Q# data types have a default value defined for them. Using the new expression with types such as qubits, operations, or functions might cause runtime errors if any array elements were not reassigned before use. To address this, Q# 0.16 introduced two new array literals, empty array and repeated constant array, and deprecated the new expression.

Chapter 3 will discuss further tools for working with arrays, such as getting the length of the array, accessing array elements, and array manipulation.

QDK libraries offer a lot of convenient functions that implement common routines for working with arrays. I will discuss the Microsoft.Quantum.Arrays library namespace in more detail in Chapter 7.

Tuples

A *tuple* is a group of a fixed number of values of potentially different types. The underlying types of the tuple elements can be any types from the Q# type system: a primitive type, a data structure, or a callable. The type of a tuple grouping types T1, T2, ..., TN is (T1, T2, ..., TN).

A tuple literal is a comma-separated list of one or more expressions, enclosed in round brackets: (expr1, expr2, ..., exprN). The expressions can be of arbitrary types.

A single-element tuple is considered the same as the underlying element, so (42) is the same as 42 or ((42)). This property is called *singleton tuple equivalence*.

You can access tuple elements using tuple deconstruction; I will discuss this in more detail in Chapter 4.

User-Defined Types

A *user-defined type* (UDT) is a tuple of anonymous and named items of different types, stored as a single data type.

User-defined types are declared inside namespaces but outside operations/functions using the keyword `newtype`, followed by the type name, the equal sign, and the tuple of UDT elements defined as types and (optionally) names:

```
newtype AnonymousPair = (Int, Bool);
newtype NamedPair = (First : Int, Second : Bool);
```

A UDT declaration generates a constructor for this type. A UDT literal can be constructed by invoking its constructor explicitly:

```
let ap = AnonymousPair(1, false);
```

You can access UDT elements as tuple elements using tuple deconstruction (see Chapter 4). Alternatively, you can use the names of the named elements (see Chapter 3).

QDK libraries offer multiple user-defined types that implement commonly used data types, both classical and quantum. The examples include `LittleEndian` and `BigEndian` for representing integers stored as qubit arrays, `Complex` and `ComplexPolar` for representing complex numbers in Cartesian and polar representations, `Fraction` and `BigFraction` for representing rational numbers, and other types. I will cover the most common library UDTs in Chapter 7.

Operations and Functions

Q# treats operations and functions similarly to the other data types. For example, you can define a variable that stores an operation, pass an operation as a parameter to another operation, or have a function return an operation as its result. We will discuss this in more detail in Chapter 5.

Conclusion

In this chapter, you've learned about the principles on which the Q# type system is built, and the data types the language offers.

In the next chapter, we will focus on the operators and expressions used to work with values of different types. After that, in Chapter 4, we will discuss Q# statements, from classical statements such as variables definition and conditional execution to purely quantum statements such as qubit allocation.

Expressions

This chapter offers an overview of the expressions defined in Q#. An *expression* is an entity that the compiler can evaluate to determine its value. Expressions are constructed from literals, variables, operations, and functions using a variety of operators, modifiers, and combinators.

In this chapter, I'll go over each type of operator, modifier, and combinator that Q# offers. Most Q# operators are very similar to those found in other languages, so I will briefly cover the syntax of the more familiar operators and spend more time on the modifiers and combinators that are less common or are unique to Q#.

I'll start with the comparative operators and operators acting on the simpler data types, such as `Bool` and `Int`, and then follow with the expressions involving more complicated data types, data structures, and finally, operations and functions.

Equality Operators

Equality operators check whether their operands are equal or not. They include equality == and inequality != operators. These operators are defined for data types Int, BigInt, Double, String, Bool, Result, Pauli, and Qubit:

```
let intEquality = (42 == 10 * 4);        // false
let stringInequality = ("hi" != "HI");   // true
```

Since most Q# types are value types, equality comparisons are done by value. The Qubit type is one exception to this rule; comparing two Qubit variables checks whether they point to the same qubit, instead of comparing the quantum states of these qubits. Two different qubits in the same state are considered to be unequal:

```
// Allocate two qubits in the |0⟩ state.
use (a, b) = (Qubit(), Qubit());
let sameStatesAreEqual = (a == b);  // false
// Copy variable b to variable c.
let c = b;
let sameQubitsAreEqual = (b == c);  // true
```

If you need to check equality of more complicated data types that don't support equality comparisons, you'll need to use library operations or implement the comparisons yourself. For example, you can check whether two arrays are equal using the

EqualA function from the `Microsoft.Quantum.Arrays` library, and you can check whether two ranges are equal by converting them to arrays using the `RangeAsIntArray` function from `Microsoft.Quantum.Convert` and then comparing those arrays (see Chapter 7 for a discussion of the QDK libraries).

Comparison Operators

Comparison operators perform quantitative comparisons on their operands, checking which of them is greater or less than the other. They include < (less than), > (greater than), <= (less than or equal), and >= (greater than or equal) operators. Comparison operators are defined only for the numeric data types `Int`, `BigInt`, and `Double`:

```
let intComparison = (42 > 13);           // true
let doubleComparison = (0.12 <= 0.11);   // false
```

Logical Operators

Q# *logical operators* and, or, and not implement the standard logical operations AND, OR, and NOT, respectively. They act on `Bool` operands and produce `Bool` results:

```
let a = false;
let b = true;
let notA = not a;    // true
let aOrB = a or b;   // true
let aAndB = a and b; // false
```

NOTE

You might see C#-style syntax for logical operators &&, ||, and ! in some of the older Q# code. This syntax has been deprecated and should not be used going forward.

As is common in other programming languages, the Q# compiler short-circuits evaluation of the operators and and or. If the first operand evaluates to `false` or `true`, respectively, the compiler will not evaluate the second operand, since it will not affect the value of the expression. If the second operand of and or or operators is an operation call, the Q# compiler will offer a compilation warning pointing out that this operation call may not be executed at runtime. Unlike C#, Q# does not have separate logical operators that force evaluation of both operands:

```
// This code will produce a compilation warning.
let b = a or DrawRandomBool(0.5);
```

Q# does not have a built-in operator for logical XOR; instead, you can use the inequality operator `!=`.

Bitwise Operators

Q# offers *bitwise* versions of AND (`&&&`), OR (`|||`), NOT (`~~~`), and XOR (`^^^`). These operators are defined for integer numeric data types `Int` and `BigInt`:

```
let a = 42;             // 42 = 0b101010
let b = 13;             // 13 = 0b001101
let aAndB = a &&& b;    //  8 = 0b001000
let aOrB  = a ||| b;    // 47 = 0b101111
let aXorB = a ^^^ b;    // 39 = 0b100111
let notA  = ~~~a;       // -43
```

The last line of this code snippet shows that bitwise negation of a positive integer produces a negative result. Similar to many classical languages, Q# uses two's complement to represent negative numbers, and inverting each bit of the positive integer includes inverting the most significant bit from 0 (used to represent zero and positive integers) to 1 (used to represent negative integers).

Q# bitwise operators also include right-shift (`>>>`) and left-shift (`<<<`) operators, which shift the binary representation of the left-hand argument right or left by the number of bits given by the right-hand argument. In other words, these operators divide or multiply the left-hand argument by the power of two defined by the right-hand argument. The left-hand argument can be of type `Int` or `BigInt`, while the right-hand argument has to be an `Int`:

```
let a = 42;        // 42 = 0b0101010
let b = a >>> 2;   // 10 = 0b0001010
let c = a <<< 1;   // 84 = 0b1010100
```

Arithmetic Operators

Q# *arithmetic operators* include addition (+), subtraction (-), multiplication (*), division (/), unary negation (-), exponentiation (^), and modulus (or remainder) (%). All these operators, except for the last one, are defined for all classical numeric data types. Modulus operator is defined for `Int` and `BigInt` data types. Arithmetic operators that have two operands require them to be of the same type, and they yield a result of the same type as the operands.

The behavior of the arithmetic operators is similar to that in other programming languages, such as C#:

```
let a = 42 / 13;    // 3
let b = 42. / 14.;  // 3.0
```

Conditional Expression

The Q# *conditional operator*, sometimes also called the ternary operator, is similar to the conditional operator `condition ? trueExpr : falseExpr` in C++ and C# or the conditional expression `trueExpr if condition else falseExpr` in Python.

The conditional expression takes the form `condition ? trueExpr | falseExpr`, where `condition` is a Boolean expression, and `trueExpr` and `falseExpr` are expressions of the same type. This expression evaluates to `trueExpr` if the condition evaluates to true, and to `falseExpr` otherwise:

```
// Generate a random Boolean value with
// 50% chance of being true and 50% - false.
let a = DrawRandomBool(0.5);
```

```
// Define another variable based on it.
let b = a ? 1 | DrawRandomInt(2, 4);
```

The Q# compiler short-circuits evaluation of the expressions trueExpr and falseExpr, evaluating only the necessary one, similarly to how it short-circuits evaluation of logical expressions. You can think of it as a convenient shorthand for the if statement (see Chapter 4); the previous code snippet is equivalent to the following code:

```
let a = DrawRandomBool(0.5);
mutable b = 0;
if a {
    set b = 1;
} else {
    set b = DrawRandomInt(2, 4);
}
```

Range Operator

You saw range operator .. in Chapter 2 when you learned about range literals of the form start..step..stop or start..stop:

```
// A range of all numbers from 1 to 10, inclusive.
let rStep1 = 1 .. 10;
// A range of odd numbers from 1 to 9, inclusive.
let rStep2 = 1 .. 2 .. 10;
```

You can also use a contextual variant of this operator (...) when the range literal defined by it is used as an index for array slicing. This variant of the range operator allows you to omit start or stop expressions, leaving them for the Q# compiler to infer (more on this later in the chapter).

String Expressions

Q# strings are used primarily for logging, rather than for string processing, so there is a very limited set of string manipulation expressions. Q# does not support string expressions that are common in general-purpose languages, such as accessing a substring or an individual character of a string, or string comparison operators.

The only operator acting on Q# strings is the *string concatenation* operator +:

```
let greeting = "Hello" + " " + "reader!";
```

The string interpolation you saw in Chapter 2 can be considered a shorthand expression that combines a series of string concatenations with calls to library functions that convert their arguments to strings. In practice, in Q#, string interpolation is used more frequently than string concatenation.

Array Expressions

You learned several array expressions in Chapter 2 when we discussed creating arrays using a new expression or various array literals:

```
let emptyArray = [];
let zeroArray = new Int[5];
let oneArray = [1, size = 3];
let arr = [1, 2, 3, 4];
```

You can use the *array item access* operator [] to access individual elements of an array. An array expression, followed by an Int expression in square brackets, will yield the array item at the given index. Q# arrays use zero-based indexing, with the element indexes starting with 0 and ending with Length(array) - 1:

```
let firstElement = arr[0];              // 1
let lastElement = arr[Length(arr) - 1]; // 4
```

Getting Array Length

The Q# code snippets in this chapter will often need to get the length of an array. Q# doesn't offer a dedicated operator for this; instead, you can use the Length function from the Microsoft.Quantum.Core namespace. We'll discuss this and the other library namespaces in detail in Chapter 7, but it's worth mentioning this function early to make the rest of this chapter easier to read.

You can use the same operator for *array slicing*, that is, getting a subarray or a subsequence of elements of the original array. An array expression, followed by a Range expression in square brackets, will yield an array composed of the elements of the original array at the indexes defined by this range:

```
// Get the first half of the array.
let firstHalf = arr[0 .. Length(arr) / 2 - 1];

// Get the elements of the array at even indexes.
let evenIndexes = arr[0 .. 2 .. Length(arr) - 1];

// Reverse the array.
let reversed = arr[Length(arr) - 1 .. -1 .. 0];
```

Note that you cannot use an array as an index for array slicing; you'll need to use a library function Subarray from Microsoft.Quantum.Arrays instead:

```
// Get the first and last elements of the array.
let ind = [0, Length(arr) - 1];
let firstAndLast = Subarray(ind, arr); // [1, 4]
```

As you write more complicated Q# code using array slicing, you'll notice that the ranges used as indexes often have 0 or Length(array) - 1 as their start or end. This observation led to Q# 0.8 introducing the *contextual* variant ... of the range operator. This operator allows you to use a shorthand instead of the typical start..step..end definition of range literals if they are used with array slicing. In this scenario, you can use ... instead of start.. or ..end (or both), and the Q# compiler will substitute 0 or Length(array) - 1 for the omitted value, depending on the step value of the range. Table 3-1 shows the values substituted for the omitted range start and range end.

Table 3-1. Interpretation of omitted start and end of the range

Range step	Omitted start	Omitted end
Positive (or not specified)	0	Length(array) - 1
Negative	Length(array) - 1	0

This allows you to rewrite the previous examples more concisely:

```
// Get the first half of the array.
let firstHalf = arr[... Length(arr) / 2 - 1];

// Get the elements of the array at even indexes.
let evenIndexes = arr[... 2 ...];

// Reverse the array.
let reversed = arr[... -1 ...];
```

Finally, *copy-and-update expressions* allow you to create a copy of an array with one or several elements replaced with new values.

A copy-and-update expression consists of the following parts:

- An array expression
- A w/ operator
- An index of type Int (to update a single element) or Range (to update several elements at once)
- A <- operator
- An expression defining the new value(s) of the array element(s). If you're updating a single element, the type of this expression should match the type of the array elements. For updating multiple elements, the expression should be an array of the same type as the array being updated:

```
// Update the first element of the array.
let firstUpdate = arr w/ 0 <- -1;
```

```
// Update all even elements of the array.
let evenUpdate = arr w/ 0 .. 2 .. 3 <- [-1, -3];
```

Note that you cannot use the open-ended range operator ...
(which you've seen used for array slicing) in this context; you
need to specify both the start and end of the range explicitly.

Copy-and-update expressions can get fairly complicated when
dealing with more complex array types, such as arrays of
arrays. In this case, you need to use nested copy-and-update
expressions. Creating a copy of a 2D array with element [i][j]
replaced will look like this:

```
let a = [[1, 2, 3], [4, 5, 6, 7]];
let (i, j) = (1, 2);
let b = a w/ i <- (a[i] w/ j <- 13);
//  b = [[1, 2, 3], [4, 5, 13, 7]];
```

This nested pair of copy-and-update expressions can be trans-
lated as "array a with its i-th element replaced with (array a[i]
with its j-th element replaced with 13)".

Copy-and-update expressions are most frequently used to
update mutable array variables (see evaluate-and-reassign statements in Chapter 4).

User-Defined Type Expressions

I discussed user-defined type (UDT) constructor expressions in
Chapter 2:

```
newtype AnonymousPair = (Int, Bool);
newtype NamedPair = (First : Int, Second : Bool);

let ap = AnonymousPair(1, false);
let np = NamedPair(2, true);
```

To access named items of a UDT, you can use the *named item
access operator* (::):

```
let fstNamed = np::First;  // 2
let sndNamed = np::Second; // true
```

The only way to access anonymous items of a UDT is by using the *unwrap operator* !, which, when applied to a variable of some user-defined type, returns a tuple of the items contained in this variable. You can combine this operator with tuple deconstruction (see Chapter 4) to access individual items of a UDT. This approach works for accessing named items of a UDT as well:

```
let nonUDTTuple = ap!; // (1, false)
let (fst, snd) = np!;  // fst = 2, snd = true
```

Finally, UDTs with named items support copy-and-update expressions similar to the ones used for arrays. These expressions allow you to create a copy of a UDT variable with some of the named items replaced with new values.

For user-defined types, a copy-and-update expression consists of the following parts:

- A UDT expression
- A w/ operator
- A name of a named item of this UDT
- A <- operator
- An expression defining the new value of the item, matching the type of this item in the UDT definition

You can chain copy-and-update expressions to update several named items at once:

```
let updFirst = np w/ First <- 3;      // (3, true)
let updBoth = np w/ First <- 4
                w/ Second <- false; // (4, false)
```

Call Expressions

A *call expression* allows you to call an operation or a function with certain parameters and to use its return value as the result of the expression evaluation. The return value of the call has to be anything other than the Unit type; as you'll see in Chapter 4, calling an operation that returns `Unit` is a statement rather than an expression:

```
let a = DrawRandomBool(0.5);
```

Lambda Expressions

Lambda expressions, also known as anonymous functions, allow you to define an operation or a function for short-term use in one code fragment, without defining a named callable visible within all code in one namespace. I'll cover the lambda expressions in Chapter 5 when discussing the functional elements of Q#.

Adjoint and Controlled Functors

Adjoint and controlled functors act on an operation that implements a unitary transformation, producing another operation that is the adjoint or controlled variant of the original operation, respectively. We'll discuss these functors in Chapter 5.

Conclusion

In this chapter, you've learned the basics of Q# expressions.

In the next chapter, we will discuss Q# statements, from classical statements such as variables definition and conditional execution to purely quantum statements such as qubit allocation. After that, in Chapter 5, we will discuss Q# operations and functions.

CHAPTER 4

Statements

This chapter offers an overview of the statements defined in Q#. A *statement* is a program instruction that describes an action to be performed. Q# is an imperative programming language, so its operations and functions are sequences of statements.

I'll start with a review of "classical" statements: variable declaration and reassignment, conditional execution, loops, calling other routines, and halting routine execution. Most other programming languages have some variants of these statements, and you're probably familiar with them conceptually, so this part focuses mostly on the syntax and any language-specific nuances.

The second part of the chapter covers statements specific to quantum programs: qubit allocation, a quantum variant of a conditional loop, and a quantum-specific flow-control construct called *conjugation*.

Example: Calculate Euler's Totient Function

Let's take a look at Example 4-1, a Q# program that calculates *Euler's totient function* of the given integer n. The value of this function equals the number of positive numbers less than or equal to n that are *coprime* to it—that is, they don't have common divisors greater than 1. This example implements the most straightforward approach to computing this function: it iterates over all numbers from 1 to n and checks whether each of them is coprime to n by calculating their greatest common divisor (GCD). This code is designed to showcase the main "classical" statements we will be considering later in this chapter.

Example 4-1. Calculating Euler's totient function in Q#

```
namespace EulersTotientFunction {
    open Microsoft.Quantum.Intrinsic; // Message

    /// # Summary
    /// Calculates Euler's totient function.
    function TotientFunction(n : Int) : Int {
        // Conditional statement checks input validity.
        if n <= 0 {
            // Fail statement throws an exception.
            fail "The argument n should be positive";
        }
        // Declare mutable variable to count coprimes.
        mutable nCoprimes = 0;
        // For loop runs through numbers from 1 to n.
        for i in 1 .. n {
            // Declare mutable variables to use when
            // computing GCD of i and n.
            mutable (x, y) = (n, i);
            // While loop runs while y is positive.
            while y > 0 {
                // Reassign both mutable variables.
                set (x, y) = (y, x % y);
            }
            // At this point x = GCD(i, n).
            // Conditional statement checks whether
            // the current number is coprime with n.
            if x == 1 {
                // Evaluate-and-reassign statement.
                set nCoprimes += 1;
```

```
            }
        }
        // Return statement.
        return nCoprimes;
    }


    @EntryPoint()
    function PrintEulersTotientFunction() : Unit {
        // Declare immutable variable - the argument
        // to use when computing the function.
        let n = 4;
        // Call statement prints the function value.
        Message($"φ({n}) = {TotientFunction(n)}");
    }
}
```

Indentation in Q# is not significant: blocks are marked explicitly using curly brackets { and }, similarly to C++ and C#, rather than using indentation, like in Python. However, the Q# style guide (*https://oreil.ly/1gtwQ*) recommends indenting blocks to improve code readability.

To compute the value of the function for other inputs, you'll need to modify this program to define a different value of n. Q# doesn't support user input during program runtime. In Chapter 6, I'll show you how to define programs that take input from the user upon their invocation, and how to pass input to them.

The part of the for loop body that calculates the greatest common divisor of two integers could be replaced with a single call to the GreatestCommonDivisorI library function from the Microsoft.Quantum.Math namespace (see Chapter 7). However, I chose to spell it out in order to include more statements in this example.

Let's take a closer look at the various statements used in this program.

Working with Variables

Q# offers multiple statements for declaring and modifying Q# variables. Before we dive into the statements themselves, I'll make some general notes about variable handling in Q# that will be important for the rest of the chapter.

Variable Scope

In general the scope of a variable defined within a statement block, such as a body of a callable or a loop body, is that statement block. Variables defined in an outer block will be visible in an inner block, but not vice versa. You cannot define a variable with a name that has already been defined earlier in the block or in an outer block; Q# prohibits this practice, which is known as *variable shadowing*.

All Q# variables are local; an attempt to define a global variable will yield a compilation error. You might have noticed that our discussion of top-level Q# elements in Chapter 1 did not include global variable declarations; this is why.

Several statements have slightly different rules that define visibility of the variables defined in them. In these cases, I'll make a separate note when discussing the corresponding statement.

Mutable and Immutable Variables

Q# has two types of variables: mutable and immutable. An *immutable variable* is effectively a constant—it's a variable that is always bound to the same value and cannot be re-bound to a different one. A *mutable variable* is a "normal" variable that can take on different values during the program execution.

Q# differentiates between mutable and immutable variables on the language level to simplify the analysis of the program behavior, so you have to declare whether the variable will be reassigned later up front. In Chapter 5, we'll see how variable mutability affects code generation performed by the Q# compiler.

Declaring Immutable Variables: let Statements

A *let statement* allows you to declare an immutable variable (that is, a constant) and to bind it to its value.

The let statement consists of the following parts:

- A let keyword
- A variable name or a tuple of names
- An equal sign
- The expression that is being bound to the variable
- A semicolon

```
let n = 10;
let doubleArray = [1., 2., 3.];
let name = "Mariia";
let gate = H;
```

The type of the variable assigned can be any type supported by Q#. Note that the let statement doesn't specify the type of the variable it defines explicitly. The type of the variable is inferred from the expression on the right side of the equal sign.

We will discuss assigning tuples separately a bit later in the chapter.

Declaring Mutable Variables: mutable Statements

A *mutable statement* allows you to declare a mutable variable (a variable that can take different values during the program execution) and bind it to its initial value.

The mutable statement consists of the following parts:

- A mutable keyword
- A variable name or a tuple of names
- An equal sign
- The expression that is being bound to the variable

- A semicolon

```
mutable m = 10;
mutable intArray = [1, 2, 3];
```

As with the let statement, the type of the variable defined using the mutable statement is inferred from the expression on the right side, and can be any type supported by Q#. The difference between the mutable and let statements comes in play with the next statement we'll look at, which allows you to reassign mutable variables.

Reassigning Mutable Variables: set Statements

A *set statement* allows you to reassign the value of a mutable variable to a different value.

The set statement consists of the following parts:

- A set keyword
- A variable name or a tuple of names
- An equal sign
- The expression that is being bound to the variable
- A semicolon

```
set m = m + 32;
set intArray = intArray + [4];
```

You cannot use the set statement with an immutable variable defined using a let statement; an attempt to do this will cause a compilation error.

Note that since Q# is a statically typed language, a set statement cannot change the type of the variable that was defined by the mutable statement. An attempt to assign a value to a variable of a different type without an explicit type cast will cause a compilation error.

Evaluate-and-reassign statements are shorthand for a special type of set statements. If the expression on the right side of the equal sign in a set statement is an application of a binary operator to the variable on the left side and another expression, you can use an evaluate-and-reassign statement to write it more concisely.

Evaluate-and-reassign statements are defined for arithmetic and bitwise binary operators, as well as string and array concatenation operators and copy-and-update expressions for arrays and UDTs. The following code snippet shows several pairs of equivalent set statements, in which the second variant is shorthand for the first variant:

```
// Increment a number by 32.
set m = m + 32;
set m += 32;

// Multiply a number by 2 using bit shift.
set m = m <<< 1;
set m <<<= 1;

// Append an element to the current array.
set intArray = intArray + [4];
set intArray += [4];

// Replace the first element of an array with 5
// using a copy-and-update expression.
set intArray = intArray w/ 0 <- 5;
set intArray w/= 0 <- 5;

// Replace an element of a UDT defined as
// newtype NamedPair = (Fst : Int, Snd : Bool);
// using a copy-and-update expression.
set np = np w/ Fst <- 3;
set np w/= Fst <- 3;
```

In order to expand an evaluate-and-reassign statement into a full set statement, the Q# compiler uses the mutable variable on the left side of the equal sign as the left-hand argument of the binary operator, and the expression on the right side of the equal sign as the right-hand argument of the binary operator. This means, for example, that you cannot use the mutable variable in an evaluate-and-reassign statement as the divisor in the division expression or the shift amount for the left-shift operator, since they are right-hand arguments of the corresponding operators.

Assigning Tuples: Tuple Deconstruction

Before moving on to different statements, let's take a closer look at assigning tuples. let, mutable, and set statements can all be applied to tuples as well as other data types. Conveniently, they are not limited to dealing with the tuple being assigned as a whole; *tuple deconstruction* allows you to deconstruct the tuple into its components and assign them to different variables separately.

Let's look at some examples that illustrate tuple deconstruction and its applications:

```
// Access tuple components separately.
let tuple = (5, false);
let (first, second) = tuple;
// first = 5, second = false

// Access tuple components that are tuples.
let nestedTuple = (42, (PauliX, 2.0));
let (n, pair) = nestedTuple;
// n = 42, pair = (PauliX, 2.0)

// Access nested tuple components.
let (n, (pauli, angle)) = nestedTuple;
// n = 42, pauli = PauliX, angle = 2.0

// Access some, but not all, components.
let (_, (pauli, angle)) = nestedTuple;

// Update two variables simultaneously.
set (x, y) = (y, x % y);

// Use library function that returns a tuple.
let (u, v) = ExtendedGreatestCommonDivisorI(a, b);
```

Note the fourth snippet that shows that you don't need to assign all components of the tuple to some variables when using tuple decomposition; you can use underscore (_) in lieu of any tuple components you don't need.

Tuple deconstruction is the only way to access unnamed tuple elements individually. Besides, it can be very convenient when working with more complicated code, since it allows you to use functions or operations that return tuples of values, arrays of tuples, and so on. The last snippet shows accessing the return value of a library function that computes the greatest common divisor of two integers a and b, represents it as a linear combination a · u + b · v = GCD(a, b), and returns a tuple (u, v).

Conditional Execution: if Statements

A *conditional statement* allows you to execute different statements depending on the values of one or several expressions. Q# offers a single if statement that implements three variants of conditional execution.

The *if statement* consists of the following parts:

- An if keyword
- A Boolean expression
- A block of statements that are executed if the expression evaluates to true

For example:

```
if n <= 0 {
    fail "The argument n should be positive";
}
```

The *if-else statement* expands the if statement, following it with an else keyword and a block of statements that are executed if the expression in the if statement evaluates to false:

```
if n % 2 == 0 {
    Message("The number is even");
```

```
    }
    else {
        Message("The number is odd");
    }
```

Finally, the *if-elif-else statement* allows you to check several conditions in a row, executing the first block for which its matching condition evaluates to `true`, and executing the optional `else` block if all conditions evaluate to `false`.

The following code snippet implements the decision-making fragment of the FooBar task, which, given an integer number, prints "Foo" if it is divisible by 3, "Bar" if it is divisible by 5, "Foobar" if it is divisible by both, and the number itself if it is divisible by neither 3 nor 5:

```
    if i % 15 == 0 {
        Message("Foobar");
    }
    elif i % 3 == 0 {
        Message("Foo");
    }
    elif i % 5 == 0 {
        Message("Bar");
    }
    else {
        Message($"{i}");
    }
```

Note that the statement blocks in each scenario must be enclosed in curly brackets, even if some of the blocks contain only a single statement. Q# doesn't allow you to omit curly brackets around the statement blocks; you'll see other examples of this later in this chapter. Enclosing the conditional expressions in round brackets is optional, though.

Remember that Q# doesn't support implicit type casts; all expressions used after `if` and `elif` keywords must be Boolean.

Loops

A *loop* allows you to execute a fragment of code repeatedly. Q#
offers three types of loops; we will start with the first two that
were featured in Example 4-1 and discuss the third one later in
the chapter.

Iterate Over a Sequence: for Loops

A *for loop* allows you to iterate over the elements of a
sequence—a range or an array—and to perform certain actions
for each element. (You cannot iterate over a tuple, since a tuple
represents a group of items of different types rather than a
sequence of items of the same type.)

The for statement consists of the following parts:

- A for keyword
- A variable or a tuple of variables
- An in keyword
- An expression that evaluates to a range or an array
- The block of statements that make up the loop body

Let's take a look at several examples of for loops and the varia-
tions in their functionality.

The simplest variant of the for loop iterates over a range of
integers. The loop variable is an integer that takes on each value
in the range in turn. Here, for example, is the Q# code for
calculating the factorial of the number n. The for loop is used
to multiply the mutable variable fact by each of the integers
from 2 to n, inclusive:

```
mutable fact = 1;
for i in 2 .. n {
    set fact *= i;
}
```

If you don't need to use the loop variable in the loop (that is, you just need to execute the loop body a certain number of times), you can replace the loop variable with an underscore (_). For example, the following code snippet calculates the nth power of 2 by multiplying the mutable variable power by 2 n times.

```
mutable power = 1;
for _ in 1 .. n {
    set power *= 2;
}
```

The second variant of the for loop iterates over the elements of an array. In this case the loop variable is of the same type as the array elements, which can be any of the types supported by Q#, from integers to data structures or even callables. This code snippet applies the Hadamard gate to each of the qubits in the array:

```
use qs = Qubit[n];
for q in qs {
    H(q);
}
```

For a more interesting example, let's apply Hadamard gates followed by different single-qubit gates with different parameters to different qubits in the array. Here, the type of the array in the for loop is ((Double, Qubit) => Unit, Double, Qubit)[], and each of its elements is a tuple of three values: a gate of type (Double, Qubit) => Unit that acts on a qubit and takes an extra floating-point parameter (see Chapter 5), a floating-point parameter to use, and a qubit to apply this gate to. Note that using tuple deconstruction when defining the loop variable allows you to define individual variables in the loop header instead of defining a tuple loop variable and deconstructing it in the loop body:

```
let gates = [Rx, Ry, Rz];
let angles = [1., 2., 3.];
use qs = Qubit[3];
let array = Zipped3(gates, angles, qs);
```

```
for (gate, angle, qubit) in array {
    H(qubit);
    gate(angle, qubit);
}
```

NOTE

This example uses a library function Zipped3, which "zips" three arrays into an array of tuples that combine respective elements of each array. Microsoft.Quantum.Arrays namespace contains a lot of very convenient functions for working with arrays (see Chapter 7).

You can replace the loop variable with an underscore when iterating over the array as well, but it is less common than when iterating over a range. In this variant you're likely to use the array elements in the loop body, rather than just use the length of the array to define the number of loop iterations. However, if your code iterates over an array of tuples, it can be convenient to replace some of the variables with underscores in tuple deconstruction if your loop body needs only part of the information stored in each tuple. For example, you could split the loop from the previous code snippet into two, applying the Hadamard gates in the first loop and the rotation gates in the second one. In this case the first loop doesn't need the information about the rotation gates you'll use in the second loop, so it can be ignored:

```
for (_, _, qubit) in array {
    H(qubit);
}
for (gate, angle, qubit) in array {
    gate(angle, qubit);
}
```

Loop variables are immutable; they are bound to each element of the sequence for the matching iteration, and go out of scope at the end of the loop body.

Q# for loops don't support transfer of control statements such as break or continue. If you anticipate the need to stop iteration early depending on some condition, use the while loop or the repeat-until loop that we'll cover later in this chapter. Alternatively, if your for loop doesn't involve allocated qubits, you can use a return statement to leave the loop and the operation/function in which it is defined.

Classical Conditional Loop: while Loops

A *while loop* allows you to evaluate an expression before each iteration and execute the loop body only if that expression evaluates to true. Note that in Q# this loop is purely classical: you can only use it within functions (recall that Q# functions can contain only classical computations). For similar functionality in operations, use the repeat-until loop we'll discuss later in this chapter.

The while statement consists of the following parts:

- A while keyword
- A Boolean expression
- A block of statements that are executed as long as the expression evaluates to true

For example, the following code snippet implements a function that finds the index of a negative element in the given array, and it returns that index or -1 if all array elements are nonnegative:

```
function FirstNegativeIndex(a : Int[]) : Int {
    mutable ind = 0;
    while ind < Length(a) and a[ind] >= 0 {
        set ind += 1;
    }
    return ind == Length(a) ? -1 | ind;
}
```

Note that, unlike in the `repeat-until` loop you'll see later, the condition of the `while` loop must be defined using variables declared outside the loop body that are updated in the loop body.

Call an Operation or a Function: Call Statements

A *call statement* allows you to call an operation or a function that returns a `Unit` value. (As you learned in Chapter 3, calling an operation or a function that returns any other type of value is a kind of expression.) For example:

```
// Calling an operation.
X(q);
// Calling a built-in function.
Message("Hello, quantum world!");
```

NOTE

Most call statements will involve calling operations. In most cases, functions are used to perform classical computations and to return the result of these computations, and thus can be used only as expressions. The few functions that return a `Unit` type and thus can be called as statements are special functions that rely on their side effects. The examples include the `Message` function you've seen in Example 4-1 and the debugging functions you'll see in Chapter 8.

We will discuss the behavior of operations and functions and calling operations in more detail in Chapter 5.

Stop Execution: return and fail Statements

Q# offers two ways to stop execution of the current operation/function, depending on whether it completed successfully or a fatal error occurred.

NOTE

Q# does not support other types of transfer-of-control statements offered by many general-purpose languages, such as break, continue, or goto.

Finish Execution: return Statements

A *return statement* signals successful completion of the current operation/function. If the signature of the callable specifies that it has a return value of type other than Unit, a return statement also returns the result of the computation. This statement stops execution of the current operation/function and returns control to the caller. If the current callable was the entry point of Q# code, the return statement returns control to the classical host program or the execution environment.

A return statement consists of the following parts:

- A return keyword
- An expression of the type that matches the return type of the current operation/function
- A semicolon

For example:

```
function FortyTwo() : Int {
    return 42;
}
```

If the callable return type is Unit, the return statement has to return the value ():

```
/// # Summary
/// Prepares the qubit in the basis state given
/// by the measurement result in computational
/// basis. The qubit starts in the |0⟩ state.
operation PrepareBasisState(
    q : Qubit,
    state : Result
) : Unit {
    if state == Zero {
        // The qubit is already in the Zero state.
        return ();
    }
    X(q);
}
```

A callable can have multiple execution paths; each must end in a return statement, except for the path that ends at the end of a callable that returns Unit, as you can see in the preceding example.

Q# imposes some restrictions on the use of return statements. You cannot use a return statement in the middle of the block that allocated qubits, but you can use it as the last statement of such a block. As long as no allocated qubits are involved, you can use a return statement at any point in the code, though you might get a "This statement will never be executed" warning for any statements after the return statement.

Throw an Exception: fail Statements

A *fail statement* signals a fatal error from which the program cannot recover. This statement halts Q# program execution completely and returns control to the classical host program or the execution environment, depending on how you run this Q# program.

Exception Handling in Q#

Unlike general-purpose languages, Q# does not offer any exception-handling mechanisms. Since Q# is a domain-specific

---

language, it doesn't provide a lot of functionality that can introduce recoverable errors. Most exceptions thrown by Q# programs indicate either a data error (for example, invalid input values) or a program error (for example, an off-by-one bug causing an `ArrayIndexOutOfBounds` exception). For simplicity, Q# propagates the exceptions all the way to the user or to the classical host code.

A `fail` statement consists of the following parts:

- A `fail` keyword
- A string—the message that will accompany the exception thrown by the statement
- A semicolon

The error message can be any expression of type `String`, including interpolated strings:

```
if n <= 0 {
    fail "The argument n should be positive";
}
```

You can use the `fail` statement at any point inside a function or an operation, including the places where you cannot use a `return` statement.

NOTE

`fail` statements are broadly used by Q# library operations and functions to ensure the constraints on their expected inputs, and in the implementation of unit tests that cover Q# libraries. They also power a lot of functions from the `Microsoft.Quantum.Diagnostics` namespace (please see Chapter 8).

Example: Prepare a Quantum State

Now let's consider Example 4-2, a Q# program that prepares a quantum state $\frac{1}{\sqrt{3}}(|00\rangle + |10\rangle + |11\rangle)$. It showcases all the remaining statements we will cover in this chapter, including all "quantum" statements.

Example 4-2. Preparing superposition state $\frac{1}{\sqrt{3}}(|00\rangle + |10\rangle + |11\rangle)$

```
namespace StatePreparation {
    open Microsoft.Quantum.Canon;        // ApplyToEach
    open Microsoft.Quantum.Diagnostics;  // DumpRegister
    open Microsoft.Quantum.Intrinsic;    // Message
    open Microsoft.Quantum.Measurement;  // MResetZ

    @EntryPoint()
    /// # Summary
    /// Prepares state (|00⟩ + |10⟩ + |11⟩) / √3.
    operation PrepareSuperpositionState() : Unit {
        // Use statement allocates the qubits.
        use (qs, aux) = (Qubit[2], Qubit());
        // Repeat-until loop runs until the loop body
        // succeeds at preparing the right state.
        repeat {
            // Call statement applies H gates to qubits
            // to prep (|00⟩ + |01⟩ + |10⟩ + |11⟩) / 2.
            ApplyToEach(H, qs);
            // Conjugation statement marks the basis
            // state we need to discard (|10⟩)
            // with |1⟩ in qubit aux.
            within {
                // Call statement applies X gate
                // to the second qubit.
                X(qs[1]);
            } apply {
                // Call statement applies controlled
                // variant of X gate to the qubits.
                Controlled X(qs, aux);
```

```
        }
        // Variable assignment statement measures
        // qubit aux and stores the result.
        let res = MResetZ(aux);
    } until res == Zero
    fixup {
        // Call statement resets qubits to |0⟩.
        ResetAll(qs);
    }
    // Call statement prints the qubits' state.
    DumpRegister((), qs);
    // Call statement resets qubits to |0⟩.
    ResetAll(qs);
    }
}
```

NOTE

As in Example 4-1, this program can be implemented
more efficiently using the ControlledOnBitString library
function from the Microsoft.Quantum.Canon namespace
to replace the within-apply statement (see Chapter 7).
However, it is spelled out here in order to include more
statements in this example.

Let's take a closer look at the new Q# statements you see in this
program.

Allocate Qubits: use and borrow Statements

The key "quantum" statement in Q# is qubit allocation. Any Q#
program always starts with no qubits and has to allocate and
release any qubits it needs.

There are two statements you can use to allocate qubits: the *use
statement* allocates fresh qubits in the |0⟩ state, and the *borrow
statement* allocates qubits that are in some other state. These
statements can appear only in operations, never in functions,

due to their inherently quantum nature. The two statements have identical syntax. The vast majority of qubit allocations in Q# programs rely on the use statement, so in this section I'll focus mostly on that, and note the subtleties of the borrow statement afterward.

The use statement consists of the following parts:

- A use keyword
- A variable name or a tuple of names
- An equal sign
- The initializer that is being bound to the variable
- A semicolon or an optional block of statements

The right side of the equal sign can have one of the limited set of initializers: Qubit() to allocate a single qubit, Qubit[n] to allocate an array of n qubits, or tuples thereof to allocate several qubits and/or qubit arrays in a single statement:

```
use q = Qubit();
...

use qs = Qubit[n];
...

use (input, output) = (Qubit[3], Qubit()) {
    // ...
}
```

The optional block of statements after the use keyword defines the *scope* of the allocated qubits: the section of the program in which they will be available. Q# doesn't have a separate "release" statement to accompany the use and borrow statements. Instead, the allocated qubits are released automatically at the end of the block in which they were allocated (in case of the simple form of the use statement) or at the end of the block that is part of the use statement, if such a block is present.

The qubits allocated with the `use` statement must be returned to the $|0\rangle$ state or measured before the release.

The compiler does not enforce this requirement. The qubits can be returned to the $|0\rangle$ state without measurement using *uncomputation*: undoing the part of the computation in which they were involved. This means that verifying their state upon release would effectively require the compiler to simulate the program during its compilation, which is not possible for programs larger than a certain (rather small) threshold. However, quantum simulators offer this verification at runtime as part of their functionality; if your code performs neither uncomputation nor measurement before returning the qubits, running it on a quantum simulator will throw a runtime error (see Chapter 6).

The `borrow` statement allocates qubits in an arbitrary unknown state and expects your program to return them to the same state before releasing them:

```
borrow q = Qubit();
// ...
// Remember to return q to its original state!
```

Under the hood, the `borrow` statement literally borrows temporarily unused qubits from other parts of the program. These qubits are not actively being used by the code that allocated them originally, so the current operation can borrow them for a bit and use them, as long as it returns the borrowed qubits to their starting state before releasing them. This means that, for example, you cannot measure the borrowed qubits—this would destroy the information about their original state and ruin the computation from which they were borrowed.

NOTE

The scenarios in which borrowed qubits can be useful are pretty advanced, and out of scope for this book. You can see the paper "Factoring using 2n+2 qubits with Toffoli based modular multiplication" (*https://oreil.ly/yXMFv*) by Thomas Häner et al. for an example of an algorithm that uses borrowed qubits to implement multicontrolled CNOT gates with few qubits.

As discussed in Chapter 2, you can define variables of Qubit data type using let and mutable statements to copy allocated qubits to new variables. However, this does not create or allocate new qubits, nor does it violate the no-cloning theorem. Instead, copying a qubit to a different variable creates another copy of the reference to the same qubit:

```
// Allocate a qubit in an unknown state.
borrow q = Qubit();
// Create another variable pointing to it.
let qCopy = q;
// Measure the copied qubit and reset it to |0⟩.
let res = MResetZ(qCopy);
// q points to the same qubit in the |0⟩ state!
```

Copying qubit variables is typically used to combine qubits from several sources—for example, combining qubits passed as an argument to an operation and auxiliary qubits allocated within that operation into a single array to be used as an argument for another operation.

Quantum Conditional Loops: repeat-until Loops

A *repeat-until loop* allows you to repeat iterations until a certain condition is satisfied. This statement can appear only in operations, and never in functions, since it is designed to work with quantum logic and conditions based on measurement results. For similar functionality in functions, use the `while` loop discussed earlier in this chapter.

The `repeat-until` statement consists of the following parts:

- A `repeat` keyword
- A block of statements that represents the loop body
- An `until` keyword
- A Boolean expression
- A semicolon or an optional `fixup` keyword followed by a block of statements that is executed after each iteration if the expression evaluated to `false` and the loop is going to restart

Here is a short example of using a `repeat-until` loop to prepare the $|1\rangle$ state without using an X gate. In it, the loop body puts a qubit in a superposition using the Hadamard gate and measures it; if the measurement yielded `Zero`, the loop repeats, but if it yielded `One`, we know that the qubit ended up in the $|1\rangle$ state:

```
use q = Qubit();
repeat {
    H(q);
    let res = M(q);
} until res == One;
```

In Example 4-2, you saw a more interesting example of a `repeat-until` loop in action:

- The loop body attempts to prepare the required state by preparing a different state using an extra qubit and measuring that extra qubit. This will prepare the required state with 75% probability and a different, incorrect state with 25% probability.

- The exit condition `res == Zero` is based on the outcome of the measurement, which tells us whether we got the required state or a different one.

- If we got a different state, the loop repeats itself after performing the `fixup` block, which resets the qubits to their starting state so that the loop body can start from a clean slate (`ResetAll(qs)`).

All parts of the loop form a single scope, so any variables defined in the loop body are visible to the expression that defines the exit condition and to the `fixup` block for the same iteration. This means, for example, that the exit condition can be defined using variables declared in the loop body, rather than mutable variables.

A `repeat-until` loop can also be used to implement a purely classical computation, as long as it happens in an operation and not in a function. But usually it's better to separate a classical computation that requires conditional iterating into a function, and to use a `while` loop instead.

Conjugation: within-apply Statements

The conjugation statement is also known as a *within-apply statement*. This statement can appear only in operations, and never in functions, due to its inherently quantum nature. It implements the pattern of applying the unitary transformations $U^\dagger V U$, where U and V are unitary transformations, and $U^\dagger$ is an *adjoint* of the transformation U: a transformation that undoes the effects of U. In terms of Q# code, the conjugation statement applies two blocks of code, U and V, followed by an automatically generated adjoint of the first block $U^\dagger$.

Unlike other language statements, conjugation is not fundamentally necessary to a quantum programming language; in fact, it was introduced to Q# only in version 0.9, almost two years after the first release! However, conjugations are ubiquitous in quantum programs, expressing concepts such as uncomputation, which returns temporarily allocated qubits to their starting states before releasing them by undoing the part of the computation in which they were involved.

Seeing how often this code pattern occurred in Q# programs, it made sense to add a special statement to the language to make writing them more convenient and less error-prone. Indeed, spelling out the adjoint transformation $U^\dagger$ manually means either forfeiting the advantages of automatic adjoint generation provided by the Q# compiler (and potentially introducing errors in the process) or having to define a separate operation for the transformation U and calling its adjoint (leading to bulkier and harder-to-read code). I will talk more about adjoints in Chapter 5.

The conjugation statement consists of the following parts:

- A within keyword
- The first block of code (transformation U)
- An apply keyword
- The second block of code (transformation V)

The following code snippet shows two equivalent fragments of code, both of which implement a *controlled-on-zero* variant of the X gate—a gate that flips the state of the target qubit if both control qubits are in the $|0\rangle$ state:

```
within {
    ApplyToEachA(X, qs);
} apply {
    Controlled X(qs, aux);
}

ApplyToEachA(X, qs);
```

```
Controlled X(qs, aux);
Adjoint ApplyToEachA(X, qs);
```

This example is too small to illustrate the advantages of using a conjugation statement instead of writing out the adjoint of the first block manually. But, as you can imagine, real-world quantum programs tend to have much more complex code in both within and apply blocks, so a conjugation statement can be really handy.

The code in the within block of a conjugation statement must be *adjointable*, i.e., it must be written in a way that allows the Q# compiler to generate its adjoint. (Note the use of library operation ApplyToEachA in the last code snippet instead of ApplyToEach; the only difference between these two operations is that ApplyToEachA has an adjoint variant defined and ApplyToEach does not.) If the within block includes any statements that don't have an adjoint specialization, the compiler will throw an error pointing to them and explaining why the adjoint cannot be generated.

Conclusion

In this chapter, you've learned everything about Q# statements, both classical and quantum ones.

In the next chapter, we will discuss Q# operations and functions, which will wrap up the first part of the book.

CHAPTER 5

Operations and Functions

This chapter dives deeper into defining and using operations and functions—the main units of Q# code.

Operations are the most general type of Q# subroutine— sequences of statements that perform a certain task, packaged as a single logical unit. *Functions* are a special type of subroutine that perform only deterministic classical computation. Together, operations and functions are called *callables*.

Since Q# is a quantum programming language, operations are much more common in Q# code—you cannot write a quantum program without using an operation. However, functions are useful in their own right, as I'll show you in this chapter.

The chapter starts with the basic ways to define functions and operations and use them, including call expressions and statements, and a description of signatures of callables.

After that I'll show how quantum gates and measurements are represented as operations in Q#, thus finishing the discussion we started in Chapter 2 of how the language expresses central quantum computing concepts. Next, I'll discuss defining and using adjoint and controlled variants of operations—powerful tools for expressing quantum algorithms more concisely.

I'll wrap up the chapter with a discussion of the functional elements of Q#, such as passing callables as arguments to other callables and using partial application to construct new callables, and the type-parameterized callables.

Defining and Using Operations and Functions: The Basics

A basic callable declaration consists of:

- An `operation`/`function` keyword that specifies whether the callable is an operation or a function
- A callable name
- A list of the callable arguments, given as a list of comma-separated pairs of the form `name : type`, wrapped in parentheses; if the callable takes no arguments, its name is followed by just the parentheses
- A colon
- A callable return type
- A callable *body*—a block of statements that are executed when the callable is called

Any callable declaration must include all these parts. Later in the chapter, I'll show you more advanced callable declarations that add several optional parts.

Example 5-1 shows how to define two Q# functions that calculate a sum and a product of two integers. Each one takes two `Int` values as an input and returns an `Int`.

Example 5-1. Defining Q# functions

```
function Sum(a : Int, b : Int) : Int {
    return a + b;
}

function Product(a : Int, b : Int) : Int {
```

```
    return a * b;
}
```

Example 5-2 shows how to define a Q# operation that applies an Ry gate to each of the qubits, using the corresponding element of the angles array as the rotation angle parameter to the gate. It takes an array of qubits and an array of floating-point numbers as an input and returns a Unit—that is, it does not produce a return value.

Example 5-2. Defining a Q# operation

```
operation ApplyRyArray(
    qs : Qubit[],
    angles : Double[]
) : Unit {
    for (q, angle) in Zipped(qs, angles) {
        Ry(angle, q);
    }
}
```

NOTE

Q# doesn't support function and operation *overloading*, or defining two callables within the same namespace with the same name and different signatures.

When you define a callable that takes a tuple as one of its arguments, you can use an alternative syntax to embed tuple deconstruction in the list of the callable arguments. The following function definitions are equivalent and demonstrate this syntax compared to the regular way of defining tuple arguments:

```
// Embed tuple deconstruction in the arguments.
function AddInputs1(
    a : Int,
    (b : Int, c : Int, d : Int),
    (e : Int, f : Int)
```

```
) : Int {
    return a + b + c + d + e + f;
}

// Define types of tuple arguments.
function AddInputs2(
    a : Int,
    t1 : (Int, Int, Int),
    t2 : (Int, Int)
) : Int {
    // Deconstruct tuple arguments in body.
    let (b, c, d) = t1;
    let (e, f) = t2;
    return a + b + c + d + e + f;
}

// Both functions are called in the same way:
let s = AddInputs1(1, (2, 3, 4), (5, 6));  // 21
```

The most straightforward way to use a function or an operation that has any return type other than Unit is through a call expression, as you saw in Chapter 3. A call expression invokes a callable with certain parameters and yields its return value that can be used later in the program:

```
let sum = Sum(5, 13);  // 18
```

The callables with Unit return type can be invoked via call statements, as you saw in Chapter 4. A call statement invokes a callable with certain parameters without producing a return value. The following code snippet uses call statements to invoke the operation ApplyRyArray and the function DumpMachine:

```
// Allocate two qubits in the |00⟩ state.
use qs = Qubit[2];
ApplyRyArray(qs, [0.5 * PI(), 0.5 * PI()]);
// Print the qubits' state to see it is
// (|00⟩ + |01⟩ + |10⟩ + |11⟩) / 2.
DumpMachine();
```

Callables that have Unit return type do not produce a meaningful return value; instead, they act through their side effects.

Since you cannot define a global variable in a Q# program, the effects of such callables are limited to changes in the state of the qubits they act on, or, in case of a small class of library functions such as Message and DumpMachine (see Chapter 8), the outputs they write to a file or some other location.

Functions limit the set of statements you can use in their bodies: you cannot call an operation from a function or use any of the quantum-specific statements (such as qubit allocation, repeat-until loop, or conjugation). Since all library primitives that implement quantum operations or draw samples from random distributions are defined as operations, this restriction ensures that functions can implement only deterministic classical computations. And since Q# doesn't support global variables and functions cannot act on qubits, function calls cannot have any side effects on the state of the program.

Operations can call any operations and functions and use any statements except the while loop, which means that they can express arbitrary computations. I'll return to the importance of the distinction between functions and operations later in this chapter, when I discuss defining adjoint and controlled variants of the quantum operations.

Signatures of Callables

The *signature* of a callable includes the types of inputs it takes and the types of outputs it produces, as well as an indication of whether the callable is an operation or a function.

More specifically, the types of inputs and the types of outputs are both described as tuples: comma-separated lists of type names enclosed in parentheses. Following the singleton tuple equivalence property (see Chapter 2), if the callable has a single input or a single output, the corresponding tuple in its signature consists of a single element and can be replaced with just the type of that input or output. The types of inputs and outputs in the signature are separated by an arrow: -> for functions or => for operations.

For example, the signature of the Sum function defined earlier in the chapter as function Sum(a : Int, b : Int) : Int is (Int, Int) -> Int, and the signature of the ApplyRyArray is (Qubit[], Double[]) => Unit. Note that the return of both these callables consists of a single value, so it is written as simply the type of the return rather than as a tuple.

You'll use callable signatures to define operations and functions that take these callables as arguments. You'll also see the callables' signatures in some error messages produced by the Q# compiler—for example, when the type of a callable passed as an argument to another callable does not match the expected type of this argument (more on that later in the chapter).

Quantum Gates and Measurements

In Chapter 2, I mentioned that quantum gates and measurements do not have corresponding primitive data types to represent them; instead, they are implemented as operations that act on qubits. Now that you are more familiar with the Q# operations, let's revisit this discussion.

Quantum gates are represented as operations that take one or several qubits as inputs and have the Unit return type. For example, the Pauli gates X, Y, and Z and the rest of the nonparameterized single-qubit gates all take one argument of type Qubit. The CNOT and SWAP gates take two arguments of type Qubit, and the CCNOT gate takes three arguments of type Qubit:

```
// Allocate two qubits in the |00⟩ state.
use qs = Qubit[2];
// Apply the Hadamard gate to the first qubit.
H(qs[0]);
// Apply the CNOT gate to the qubits.
CNOT(qs[0], qs[1]);
// The state is now (|00⟩ + |11⟩)/√2.
```

Some operations that represent quantum gates can take non-qubit inputs in addition to their qubit arguments. For example, the rotation gates Rx, Ry, and Rz all take two arguments,

requiring a rotation angle of type Double in addition to the qubit argument:

```
// Allocate a qubit in the |0⟩ state.
use q = Qubit();
// Apply Ry gate.
Ry(0.5, q);
// The state is now 0.97|0⟩ + 0.25|1⟩.
```

Quantum measurements are typically represented as operations that take one or several qubits as inputs and have the return type Result or Result[]. The most commonly used measurement, measurement in the computational basis, is implemented as the operation M, which takes one argument of type Qubit and returns a value of type Result:

```
use q = Qubit();
Ry(0.5, q);
// Measure the qubit.
let m = M(q);
// Yields Zero with probability 94%
// and One with probability 6%.
```

The extension of this operation, MultiM, takes one argument of type Qubit[] and returns a value of type Result[], which will be an array of results of the measurements performed on each qubit:

```
use qs = Qubit[2];
H(qs[0]);
CNOT(qs[0], qs[1]);
let ms = MultiM(qs);
// Yields [Zero, Zero] with probability 50%
// and [One, One] with probability 50%.
```

Similarly to quantum gates, operations that represent measurements can take inputs that are not qubits. For example, the operation Measure, which represents joint measurements in Pauli bases, takes two arguments: an array of qubits that are measured and an array of Pauli values that specifies the bases for the measurement:

```
use qs = Qubit[2];
H(qs[0]);
CNOT(qs[0], qs[1]);
let parity = Measure(qs, [PauliZ, PauliZ]);
// Yields Zero with probability 100%.
```

The examples in this section use built-in gates and measurements from the Microsoft.Quantum.Intrinsic and Microsoft.Quantum.Measurement namespaces; I'll discuss these namespaces further in Chapter 7. However, you can also define your own operations for quantum gates and measurements if you need them. For example, Ising coupling gates are implemented natively in some trapped-ion quantum computer architectures, but they are not built-in gates for Q#; if you want to use these gates in your code, you'll need to define operations to implement them yourself.

NOTE

You cannot necessarily deduce whether a certain operation implements a quantum gate (that is, a unitary transformation), a measurement, or neither based on its signature alone. For example, the library operation Reset takes a qubit as an input and has a Unit return type, same as a quantum gate would, but internally it performs a measurement to reset the qubit to the $|0\rangle$ state. Grover's search algorithm can be represented as an operation that takes qubits as inputs and returns an array of measurement results, but it is not considered a measurement operation.

Defining and Using Adjoint and Controlled Specializations of Operations

Unitary transformations (that is, quantum gates of varying levels of complexity) have adjoint and controlled variants. An *adjoint variant* of a unitary transformation U is its inverse—a transformation denoted as $U^\dagger$ that undoes the effects of U. A *controlled variant* of a unitary transformation U offers a quantum analogue of conditional execution in which the unitary U is applied to one group of qubits (*target qubits*) depending on the state of another group of qubits (*control qubits*). More specifically, it's a transformation that applies U to the target qubits only if the control qubits are in the $|1\rangle$ state. Both adjoint and controlled constructs are extremely commonly used to express quantum algorithms, so it is a very good idea for a quantum programming language to offer convenient tools to work with both variants.

Q# allows you to include information about the adjoint and controlled variants of operations in their definitions in order to make them easy to define and access. In Q#, adjoint and controlled variants are called *specializations* of operations.

NOTE

The definition of adjoint and controlled specializations makes sense only for operations that return Unit type. Functions or operations with non-Unit return types cannot support these specializations.

To specify that an operation has an adjoint specialization, a controlled specialization, or both, you add the information about operation *characteristics* to the operation definition, after its return type and before its body. Table 5-1 shows the syntax of specifying the operation characteristics.

Table 5-1. Specifying characteristics of a Q# operation

Suffix	Meaning
is Adj	Operation has an adjoint specialization.
is Ctl	Operation has a controlled specialization.

Suffix	Meaning
is Adj + Ctl	Operation has both an adjoint and a controlled specialization, as well as their combination, controlled adjoint specialization.

The `ApplyRyArray` operation from Example 5-2 can have both specializations defined, so you can add the suffix is Adj + Ctl to its definition to express that:

```
operation ApplyRyArray(
    qs : Qubit[],
    angles : Double[]
) : Unit is Adj + Ctl {
    for (q, angle) in Zipped(qs, angles) {
        Ry(angle, q);
    }
}
```

Operation characteristics are included in the signature of that operation as well. Similarly to operation definitions, the characteristics suffix is appended to the signature after the return type of the operation. The signature of `ApplyRyArray`, for example, becomes (Qubit[], Double[]) => Unit is Adj + Ctl.

Using Operation Specializations

You can access operation specializations using the adjoint and controlled *functors* mentioned in Chapter 3. These functors take an operation that supports the corresponding specialization and produce another operation—the implementation of that specialization.

The expression `Adjoint op` produces an operation that implements the adjoint specialization of operation `op`. This operation takes the same arguments as the original operation:

```
use qs = Qubit[2];
let angles = [.2, .4];
Adjoint ApplyRyArray(qs, angles);
```

The expression `Controlled op` produces an operation that implements the controlled specialization of operation `op`. This operation takes two arguments: the first one is an array of control qubits, and the second one is a tuple of the arguments of the original operation. In the following code snippet, the array `cs` acts as the control, and `qs` as the target qubits:

```
use (cs, qs) = (Qubit[1], Qubit[2]);
H(cs[0]);
let angles = [.2, .4];
Controlled ApplyRyArray(cs, (qs, angles));
```

Note that the first argument of the controlled specialization is always an array of qubits; if you need to implement a gate with a single qubit as a control, you'll use a single-qubit array as a parameter. Calling a controlled specialization of an operation with an empty array of qubits as the controls is equivalent to calling the operation itself unconditionally. If the original operation took a single parameter, you can take advantage of singleton tuple equivalence to pass the same parameter as the second argument of its controlled specialization, without converting it into a tuple.

The operations produced by both adjoint and controlled functors support the same specializations as the original operation. You can apply multiple functors in a row to an operation; the compiler will simplify the resulting expression when required. For example, `Adjoint Adjoint op` will be simplified to `op`, since any unitary is the adjoint of its own adjoint. `Controlled Controlled op` will be simplified to `Controlled op` with an extended set of control qubits. Any other sequences of mixed adjoint and controlled functors will be converted to `Controlled Adjoint op`.

Generating Operation Specializations Automatically

Very often, adding the characteristics suffix to the operation definition is enough to specify the behavior of its specialization! By default, the Q# compiler will generate the specialization automatically based on the characteristics you've added, without you having to spell them out by hand.

NOTE

This section offers some insight into the internals of the Q# compiler. It is not strictly necessary for writing Q# programs, but understanding this topic will help you troubleshoot some rather confusing issues and ultimately write more elegant code.

How does the Q# compiler generate the specializations? To generate the adjoint specialization, it breaks up the operation body into individual statements, reverses their order, and uses the adjoint of each statement recursively.

Let's take a look at several examples:

- A sequence of call statements reverses the order of statements, and each operation call is replaced with a call of its adjoint specialization. Note that this means that each operation called within the body must have its adjoint defined.

- An if statement keeps its structure, with the bodies of each conditional branch replaced with their adjoints.

- A for loop reverses the order of iteration, and the loop body is replaced with its adjoint.

- Some statements, such as immutable variable definition and qubit allocation, remain unchanged. This includes call expressions that evaluate functions; since functions implement only deterministic computations without side effects on the rest of the computation, you can use the same function call with the same parameters in the adjoint of the operation and it will be guaranteed to produce the same return value.

The process to generate the controlled specialization is similar: the compiler breaks up the operation body into individual statements and uses the controlled specialization of each statement recursively. Similarly, each operation called within the body must have its controlled specialization defined.

Generating the controlled adjoint specialization combines these two approaches: the compiler reverses the order of individual statements and uses the controlled adjoint specialization of each statement recursively.

Note that a lot of language constructs make it impossible to generate the adjoint or controlled variants of the code that uses them automatically. These include:

- Measurements, or, more generally, operations that have any return type other than Unit
- Calling operations without a defined corresponding specialization
- Mutable variables
- Repeat-until loops

It is possible to work around some of these limitations. In particular, the mutable variables in the operation you need to invert often are classical and updated only via a deterministic classical computation (for example, if you're using them to calculate the number of loop iterations done by a for loop). In this case, you can refactor your code to extract all the computations that update the mutable variables into a separate function and then call that function from the operation. You can find an example of such a refactoring in the supplemental materials repository (*https://oreil.ly/5wHUB*).

Defining Operation Specializations Manually

Sometimes automatically generating adjoint and controlled
specializations is impossible or yields a suboptimal result.

The first scenario occurs if the operation body is implemented
using prohibited language constructs, but the operation still
implements a valid unitary transformation and thus can have
both specializations. You can find an example of such an operation in the supplemental materials repository (*https://oreil.ly/
OEgf2*).

In these cases you can define the necessary specializations
explicitly, using your knowledge of the transformation the
operation implements and the optimizations that can be
applied to define the specializations.

Example 5-3 shows an example of defining specializations
explicitly. We'll use the operation ApplyRyArray again.

Example 5-3. Defining operation specializations explicitly

```
operation ApplyRyArray(
    qs : Qubit[],
    angles : Double[]
) : Unit is Adj + Ctl {
    body (...) {
        for (q, angle) in Zipped(qs, angles) {
            Ry(angle, q);
        }
    }
    adjoint (...) {
        // The gates applied to different qubits
```

```
        // commute, so no need to reverse loop.
        for (q, angle) in Zipped(qs, angles) {
            // Adjoint of a rotation gate is
            // the same gate with the opposite
            // rotation angle.
            Ry(-angle, q);
        }
    }
    controlled (cs, ...) {
        for (q, angle) in Zipped(qs, angles) {
            Controlled Ry(cs, (angle, q));
        }
    }
    controlled adjoint auto;
}
```

You'll notice several new syntax elements:

- The body keyword defines the block of code that implements the body of the operation, that is, the operation itself without any specializations. The ellipsis (...)
  instructs the Q# compiler to copy the arguments from the
  operation declaration and use them as the arguments for
  the operation body, as well as for implementing the specializations. The argument to any user-defined specialization must be of the form ...; you cannot repeat arguments
  here.

- The adjoint specialization uses the same list of arguments
  as the operation itself, while the controlled specialization
  uses an extra argument, cs, which provides an array of
  control qubits. Since controlled specializations are always
  controlled on a qubit array, you don't need to specify the
  type of this argument.

- The Q# compiler assumes that the array of control qubits
  can have an arbitrary size. If you need to define the controlled specialization only for arrays of certain sizes, you
  will have to implement this restriction in the code of the
  controlled block.

- You can use *autogeneration directives* to mix and match explicitly defined specializations with automatically generated ones. For example, you can use the `adjoint self` directive to specify that the operation is self-adjoint—that is, that the compiler should use the body of the operation as its adjoint. You can also use the `auto` directive to instruct the compiler to generate this specialization automatically. In Example 5-3, the `controlled adjoint auto` directive indicates that this specialization should be generated based on the provided controlled and adjoint specializations. Autogeneration directives appear on their own, without an accompanying code block.

NOTE

Defining operation specialization manually is a fairly advanced topic and is not something you're likely to do on a daily basis. This section briefly outlines the basics; for more details, see the Q# documentation (*https://oreil.ly/souUS*).

Functional Elements of Q#

I've mentioned that Q# treats operations and functions as just another kind of data type—one that is defined differently but can be used in many similar ways. Let's take a closer look at the scenarios in which Q# callables behave like data types.

Callable-Typed Variables

To start with, you can define and use a variable of any callable type, much like you'd use variables of other types:

```
let statePrep = ApplyRyArray;
```

Once you've defined a variable of a callable type, you can use it to call that callable just as you would use the callable name itself, passing it the parameters and receiving its return, if needed:

```
use qs = Qubit[2];
let angles = [.2, .4];
statePrep(qs, angles);
```

You can also use callable types as part of data structures, including tuples, arrays, and user-defined types:

```
// An array of functions that act on two integers.
let binaryIntFunctions = [Sum, Product];
// Evaluate each function for the given inputs.
for op in binaryIntFunctions {
    Message($"{op(5, 13)}");
}
```

You can use callables as values in some types of expressions beyond call expressions. The following example shows two equivalent ways to calculate a sum or a product of two integers, depending on a Boolean parameter:

```
// Choose whether to calculate sum or product.
let calcSum = true;
let (a, b) = (5, 13);

// Choose between two integer expressions.
let res1 = calcSum ? Sum(a, b) | Product(a, b);

// Choose between two functions and
// evaluate the chosen function.
let func = calcSum ? Sum | Product;
let res2 = func(a, b);
```

Q# supports a rather limited set of expressions for callables. You can use them in string interpolation expressions (though any callable converted to a string is just its name, without its namespace or signature) and in ternary expressions, but you cannot, say, compare them using the equality operator (see Chapter 3).

Already you can imagine that these capabilities of Q# callables can be useful. For example, perhaps you have a complicated test that you want to run against each of a set of operations (say, all primitive gates). You can avoid duplicating code by defining an array of the gates you want to test and running a for loop over it to repeat the test for each of the array elements.

Using Callables as Arguments

You can define callable-typed arguments for other callables. You cannot specify simply "a function" argument, though; you need to use a specific callable signature as the type of this argument so that the Q# compiler knows exactly what callables can be passed as this parameter and in which contexts they can be used.

Example 5-4 shows how you can define a function that "reduces" a given array of integers by applying the given function to the first two elements of the array, then to the result of that and the third element, then to the result of that and the fourth element, and so forth. In other words, this function calculates f(…f(f(array[0], array[1]), array[2]), …).

Example 5-4. Reduce function

```
function Reduce(
    array : Int[],
    f : (Int, Int) -> Int
) : Int {
    if Length(array) == 0 {
        fail "Undefined result for empty array.";
    }
    mutable res = array[0];
    // Iterate through all array elements,
    // starting with the second one.
    for a in array[1 ...] {
        set res = f(res, a);
    }
    return res;
}
```

Now you can pass the name of the function you want to use for reducing as an argument to Reduce. Alternatively, you can pass any expression that produces a function of the right type, such as a lambda expression (more on that later):

```
let array = [1, 2, 3, 4];
let product = Reduce(array, Product);      // 24
let sum = Reduce(array, (a, b) -> a + b); // 10
```

You cannot pass an operation instead of a function or vice versa, even if they have identical arguments and return types. For example, if you attempt to pass an operation instead of a function as the second argument of Reduce and it otherwise matches the required function signature, you'll get the following compilation error:

```
The type ((Int, Int) -> Int) does not match
the type ((Int, Int) => Int).
Expected type: ((Int, Int) -> Int)
Actual type:   ((Int, Int) => Int)
```

The callable you pass as a parameter has to match the signature of the argument precisely, with one exception: an operation parameter is allowed to have more specializations than specified in the signature of the argument. If the argument is specified as Qubit[] => Unit, you can pass operations that have adjoint and/or controlled specifications as this argument. But if the argument is specified as Qubit[] => Unit is Adj, you can't pass operations that don't have adjoint specification (but you can pass operations that have both adjoint and controlled specifications).

Within the operation body, you'll have access only to the specifications of the argument that are specified in the signature of the argument.

Being able to use callables as arguments to other callables is a powerful tool for implementing quantum programs. A lot of quantum algorithms take quantum operations of varying complexity as parameters. They include any algorithms that are expressed in terms of quantum oracles, starting with the famous Deutsch-Jozsa algorithm and Grover's search algorithm, as well as phase estimation, amplitude amplification, and other tools commonly used as building blocks for more complicated algorithms. If you couldn't pass a quantum operation as a parameter to such an algorithm, you would have to implement it from scratch every time you needed to use it, leading to a lot of code duplication and bugs.

Partial Application

Partial application refers to defining a new callable by taking an existing one and providing one or several of its parameters. The rest of the arguments of the original callable become the arguments of the new one.

For example, we can use the function Sum and fix its first parameter to equal 1 to define a new function called increment:

```
let increment = Sum(1, _);
let three = increment(2);
```

The syntax used to define a new callable using partial application is similar to the call expression syntax. You provide the list of callable parameters in parentheses after the callable name, providing the parameters you fix as values or expressions, and replacing the omitted parameters with an underscore.

The result of partial application is a callable that takes as its inputs a list of arguments that were omitted when defining it. When invoked, this callable combines the parameters provided with the call with the parameters provided in its definition to get the full list of arguments. It then invokes the original callable with these parameters and returns the result.

The function defined in the previous code snippet is equivalent to the following one:

```
function Increment(b : Int) : Int {
    return Sum(1, b);
}
```

The signature of the callable defined using partial application matches the signature of the original callable, except that it drops the arguments that were provided. So functions remain functions and operations remain operations, and operations that had certain specializations defined keep them. The shape of the arguments is also maintained; a tuple argument with some of the elements provided becomes a tuple argument with fewer elements (unless there is only one element remaining, in which case singleton tuple equivalence allows you to replace the tuple with the type of that element). Note that if the callable takes a user-defined type argument, it needs to be either fixed or carried over as an argument to the new callable; you cannot use partial application to fix some, but not all, of the UDT elements.

Partial application is another convenient tool when implementing quantum algorithms, though, unlike being able to pass callables as arguments to other callables, the effects of partial application can be imitated without using the actual syntax.

Let's consider Grover's search algorithm—a "framework" algorithm that takes an operation with signature `(Qubit[], Qubit) => Unit` (the quantum oracle) as a parameter. However, the oracle implementation can take additional parameters; for example, an oracle that checks whether a number is a solution of an equation will take the coefficients of that equation as arguments alongside the qubit parameters. Partial application allows you to create a generic oracle implementation and then define an oracle to solve a given problem by fixing those problem-specific parameters before passing that oracle to the library implementation of Grover's search.

Lambda Expressions

Sometimes you need to define a small simple callable to use it just once—typically to pass it as a parameter to another callable, such as the Reduce function in Example 5-4. *Lambda expressions*, introduced to Q# in version 0.23, provide a lightweight way to do that without the overhead of defining a named callable.

A lambda expression consists of the following parts:

- A list of the callable arguments, given as a tuple of argument names
- An arrow that denotes the type of the callable, either -> for a function or => for an operation
- A callable body: a single call statement that defines the operation or an expression that specifies the function's return value

For example, the function Sum from Example 5-1 can be defined much more concisely as follows:

```
let sum = (a, b) -> a + b;
```

The operation ApplyRyArray from Example 5-2 can be rewritten in the following way:

```
let applyRyArray = (qs, angles) =>
    ApplyToEachCA(Ry, Zipped(qs, angles));
```

Lambda expressions cannot include blocks of code or any types of statements besides call statements. To express the same functionality as the for loop used in the operation Apply RyArray, the lambda expression has to use two library functions that you haven't encountered before. ApplyToEachCA applies the

---

operation given by the first argument to each element of the array given by the second argument. Zipped "zips" together two arrays, producing an array of tuples that consist of their matching elements. You'll learn more about the QDK libraries in Chapter 7.

Note that, unlike the full named callable definitions, lambda expressions don't specify the types of their arguments or outputs explicitly. Instead, the Q# compiler infers these types, either from the body of the lambda expression or from its first use.

For the previous code snippet, the Q# compiler can figure out the type of the variable applyRyArray even if it is not used later in the code. The operation Ry requires arguments of types Qubit and Double, so qs and angles must be arguments of types Qubit[] and Double[], respectively, for this lambda expression to make sense.

On the other hand, defining the variable sum without using it yields a compilation error. Q# has multiple types that support addition, so the compiler cannot figure out which of these types should be used in this function's signature—a string, an array, or one of the numeric types. However, once you use this variable (for example, to pass it to Reduce together with an array of integers), the compiler will be able to resolve its type.

For an operation defined as a lambda expression, the compiler has to figure out not just the type of its inputs and outputs but also any specializations it has. The operation will have all specializations that can be generated automatically from its body, that is, the same ones as the operation used in the call statement. In our example, the variable applyRyArray will have the signature (Qubit[], Double[]) => Unit is Adj + Ctl, since it's defined via a call to ApplyToEachCA, which has both adjoint and controlled specializations defined.

Similar to partial application, lambda expressions are a type of expression. You can use them to define a local callable-typed variable or to pass a value directly to a callable, but not to define a callable visible at the namespace level.

The body of a lambda expression has access to all callables defined in the same namespace and in the open namespaces, as well as to all variables defined before the lambda expression. You've already seen a lambda expression defined using library functions, which relies on the corresponding namespaces being open. As another example, you can define an operation that applies the Ry gate with the same angle parameter to an array of qubits as follows:

```
// Define a variable.
let angle = PI();
// Use variable in the lambda expression body.
let applyRyFixedAngleArray = (qs) =>
    ApplyToEachCA(Ry(_, angle), qs);
```

Lambda expressions are typically used to define single-line callables that are not reused outside a local code fragment. If a callable is used multiple times in several places in your code, you might prefer to define it as a named callable, since this allows you to avoid code duplication and to simplify future maintenance.

Defining and Using Type-Parameterized Callables

Q# allows you to define *type-parameterized callables*, similar to generics in C#. A lot of algorithms work the same regardless of the data type they're processing. Type-parameterized callables allow you to implement such algorithms for a generic case and then call them with a specific type parameter in each particular case.

A callable declaration can specify one or several *type parameters*, which are then used to specify the types of the callable's inputs and/or outputs. Type parameters are specified in angle brackets between the name of the callable and the parentheses that contain the list of its input parameters. The name of each type parameter must start with a tick (').

For example, consider the following example of a type-parameterized function that converts an argument to a string and appends a prefix to it:

```
function ToStringWithPrefix<'T>(
    a : 'T,
    prefix : String
) : String {
    return $"{prefix} {a}";
}
```

The function ToStringWithPrefix has one type parameter 'T—the type of the argument that is converted to a string—and two input parameters, one of them of type 'T. The other input parameter and the output have type String, which doesn't depend on the type parameter.

Now the other callables can call ToStringWithPrefix with values of different types used as the first argument. In each case the Q# compiler will be able to deduce the type used as 'T based on the type of the value used, and to generate a suitable implementation based on this type:

```
Message(ToStringWithPrefix("World", "Hello"));
Message(ToStringWithPrefix(5, "N ="));
```

It is possible to provide the type of the type parameter explicitly when calling the type-parameterized callables, but in most cases it is not necessary. If you choose to do so, you need to provide the type name(s) in angle brackets between the name of the callable and the parentheses that contain the list of its inputs:

```
Message(ToStringWithPrefix<Int>(5, "N ="));
```

Type-parameterized callables can use types derived from their type parameters as well. For example, this function takes an array of type 'T and returns an array of all its elements with even indexes:

```
function EvenElements<'T>(a : 'T[]) : 'T[] {
    return a[... 2 ...];
}
```

Type-parameterized callables can also have multiple type parameters. For example, the following function takes a two-element tuple as an input and returns a tuple with its elements swapped:

```
function TSwap<'T, 'S>(
    tuple : ('T, 'S)
) : ('S, 'T) {
    let (t, s) = tuple;
    return (s, t);
}
```

In this case, we could've used the singleton tuple equivalence property to simplify the function definition to take two individual parameters instead of one tuple parameter:

```
function TSwap<'T, 'S>(
    t : 'T,
    s : 'S
) : ('S, 'T) {
    return (s, t);
}
```

The capabilities of Q# type-parameterized callables are narrower than, say, those of C++ templates. Since Q# doesn't support operator overloading, you cannot define, for example, the following type-parameterized function to return the minimum of two arguments:

```
// This code produces a compilation error
// "Type 'T does not support arithmetic operators".
function Min<'T>(a : 'T, b : 'T) : 'T {
    return a < b ? a | b;
}
```

This function definition produces a compilation error, since the Q# compiler cannot guarantee that the type 'T supports the comparison operator. To implement a function that performs more complicated computations on type-parameterized inputs, pass any operators you'll need to work with the type parameters as the arguments to the callable, alongside the actual values it will process. The following example rewrites the function Min to take an additional parameter—a comparison function lessThan:

```
open Microsoft.Quantum.Logical;

function Min<'T>(
    a : 'T, b : 'T,
    lessThan : ('T, 'T) -> Bool
) : 'T {
    return lessThan(a, b) ? a | b;
}

let minI = Min(1, 2, (a, b) -> a < b);    // 1
let minD = Min(.2, .1, (a, b) -> a < b);  // 0.1
```

You can use partial application with type-parameterized callables to define new callables, but you need to either provide type parameters explicitly or fix the arguments that allow the Q# compiler to figure out the types of all type parameters. You cannot define new type-parameterized callables using partial application.

To illustrate this, let's extend the earlier example of a function ToStringWithPrefix to take two arguments of the same type:

```
function ToStrWithPrefix2<'T>(
    a : 'T,
    b : 'T,
    prefix : String
) : String {
    return $"{prefix} {a} {b}";
}
```

You can define a new function by fixing the first or the second parameter, which allows the compiler to figure out the type of the other parameter:

```
let f = ToStrWithPrefix2(2, _, _);
// Signature (Int, String) -> String
```

But you cannot define a new function by fixing the third parameter, unless you provide the type of the type parameter explicitly:

```
let f = ToStrWithPrefix2<Int>(_, _, "Hi");
// Signature (Int, Int) -> String
```

I'll show you more examples of type-parameterized functions in Chapter 7 when we discuss the `Microsoft.Quantum.Arrays` namespace.

Conclusion

With this chapter we wrap up the first part of the book, which discussed the Q# language and writing Q# programs. In the second part, the focus shifts to the Microsoft Quantum Development Kit, showing you how to use the tools it provides to work with your Q# programs. I'll start by discussing quantum software development workflow at large and then show you different ways to run Q# programs.

Using the Microsoft Quantum Development Kit

CHAPTER 6

Running Q# Programs

This chapter starts by discussing the structure of quantum applications and the typical stages of the quantum software development process. Some of these steps you'll recognize from classical software development, and some are uniquely quantum.

After that I introduce *quantum simulators*—tools commonly used for testing and evaluating quantum programs prior to running them on quantum hardware. Quantum simulators are an integral part of quantum software development workflows, and understanding their capabilities and role will be essential for the rest of this book.

The main part of this chapter describes the various ways to run Q# programs, on their own or interwoven with classical programs, in different environments, and the ways to choose the best environment for your purposes.

Quantum Applications

Quantum computers are often considered to be a type of *coprocessor*—a specialized processor used to augment the functions of the main processor. A coprocessor, such as a GPU, performs certain kinds of processor-intensive tasks, like graphics acceleration, better than the main processor, and offloading those tasks to the coprocessor can improve overall system performance. Similarly, quantum computers will offer quantum speedups for certain types of problems, but by no means for all of them.

Most quantum computing applications will use a hybrid workflow, combining classical and quantum code. This way, the quantum computer solves the computationally heavy subtasks it is best suited for, and the classical computer handles the rest of the subtasks, such as interacting with the user, querying databases, preparing the data for the quantum subtask, and so on. Q# emphasizes this separation of quantum and classical code: being a domain-specific language, it doesn't support a lot of functionality that general-purpose languages offer, such as reading data from a file or accepting user input. Figure 6-1 shows a typical workflow of one such hybrid application and the task separation between its classical and quantum components.

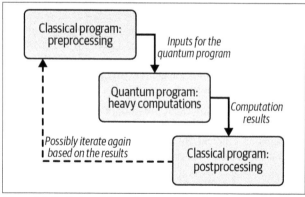

Figure 6-1. Typical workflow of a quantum application

Examples of Algorithms Combining Quantum and Classical Steps

A lot of educational resources on quantum computing focus on smaller examples of quantum algorithms that don't require integration with classical software, skipping some essential steps of this workflow. Let's consider several examples of quantum algorithms that combine quantum and classical components, thus serving as a better illustration for this workflow.

Some quantum chemistry applications rely on evaluating the *ground state energy* of a molecule—the lowest possible energy among all configurations of that molecule. The input to the quantum part of such an application will include a description of the structure of the molecule that needs to be modeled. This description can be very complicated, and most likely you'll produce it using classical chemistry simulation packages. In this case, your application's workflow will include several steps:

- Selecting the molecule to work with
- Generating its detailed description using specialized classical software
- Finding the ground state energy of the molecule
- Postprocessing the result to produce human-readable conclusions

Another good example of a quantum algorithm that relies on classical postprocessing is *Simon's algorithm*—an algorithm that analyzes a class of 2-to-1 functions to identify the bit strings that describe them. The algorithm runs the quantum circuit multiple times to assemble a system of linearly independent equations, and then proceeds to solve this system classically.

This means that Q# programs often need to be tightly integrated with code written in classical programming languages, so as to make this hybrid workflow as smooth and easy to implement as possible.

Quantum Software Development

A typical development process for this kind of hybrid quantum-classical application is shown in Figure 6-2.

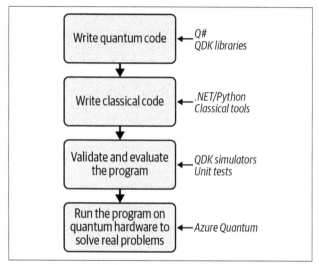

Figure 6-2. Quantum software development process

In Part I of this book we focused on the first step of the process, discussing the Q# language and the fundamentals of writing quantum code with it. However, the code you'll write with that knowledge alone is likely to be fairly low level, and you'll have to develop it from scratch. The QDK offers a rich collection of Q# libraries that implement a lot of building blocks commonly used in quantum programs, allowing you to keep your code high level and to focus on the logic of your algorithm. In Chapter 7, we will discuss Q# libraries in more detail.

You can see that the quantum software development process includes writing both quantum and classical code, the first and second steps of the process. Sometimes, if your application is extremely simple and does not require heavy pre- or postprocessing, you can get away with skipping the classical code altogether, but in most practical applications the classical part will play a significant role. In this chapter, we'll discuss the tools you can use to integrate your Q# code with classical code. I won't talk about developing classical code more generally, since it's a much broader topic than can fit in one chapter!

The third step of the process involves using a variety of tools to validate and evaluate your quantum program to make sure that (1) it is correct and (2) it is viable to run on a quantum computer you have access to. This is an extremely important step, especially in the current era, when the small sizes of available quantum devices set hard limitations on the scale of the quantum programs you can run on them, and their scarcity demands that you debug your programs before you run them on hardware. In this chapter, I'll only introduce the tools available for running Q# programs locally on your classical computer, since they are essential for the discussion of running Q# programs in general. We will discuss testing and debugging tools and techniques in greater detail in Chapter 8.

The fourth and final step of the quantum software development process is running your application on a quantum computer. Q# applications are designed to run on *Azure Quantum* (*https://oreil.ly/9YKIB*), Microsoft's cloud ecosystem supporting quantum computing. Using Azure Quantum is out of scope of this book; it is a young ecosystem, and the pool of tools and services it offers is growing rapidly.

Quantum Simulators

Before we dive deeper into the various scenarios of running Q# code, let's talk about a set of tools that turn out to be extremely useful for quantum software development—*quantum simulators*. Quantum simulators are classical programs that allow you to run small simulations of quantum systems and thus to execute quantum programs without access to quantum hardware.

A typical quantum software development process will use simulators to validate and evaluate programs before running them on quantum hardware.

The QDK includes multiple quantum simulators that serve different purposes. Let's look at each one in turn.

Full State Simulator

The *full state simulator* performs mathematically accurate simulation of the quantum gates and measurements applied by your program to the qubits it allocates. (In the literature this type of simulator is referred to as a *state vector simulator*.)

Internally, the full state simulator represents the quantum state of the program as a vector of complex numbers—the amplitudes of the basis states of the system. Quantum gates change those amplitudes following the rules for matrix multiplication. The simulator performs measurements by choosing a random measurement outcome based on the outcome probabilities computed using the amplitudes and then adjusting the state of the system to match the measurement result to reflect the "collapse" of the state caused by the measurement.

The full state simulator is a perfect replacement for an actual quantum computer—up to a certain point. Allocating each extra qubit doubles the number of the amplitudes that describe the system and thus the amount of memory required to store the full state of the quantum system, as long as the system is entangled. It also increases the time required to apply each individual gate, since in entangled systems applying a single gate might involve updating every amplitude. This means that while an average laptop can easily run the full state simulator for programs of 20–30 qubits, simulating over 45 qubits can require concerted efforts of a whole computer cluster, and simulating a general program that uses several hundreds of qubits is well beyond the capabilities of the world's aggregate classical computational power!

In practice, the full state simulator is widely used to validate and verify programs. In addition to the program state simulation, this simulator performs a broad range of runtime checks. Some of these checks are similar to the runtime checks done in classical programming; for example, checking that your program doesn't access any qubits that have already been released is similar to detecting classical memory-access errors. Others are quantum specific, such as checking that the same qubit is not used as both a control and a target for a controlled gate.

One of the runtime checks the full state simulator does is the check for the released qubits not being entangled with the qubits still in use. Up through version 0.11, the released qubits were required to be in the $|0\rangle$ state, but version 0.12 relaxed this requirement to allow releasing the qubits that were measured immediately before the release.

Qubits are a very limited resource in quantum computers, and we expect them to remain scarce for quite some time to come. This means that the runtime for quantum programs is designed to reuse the temporarily allocated qubits as much as possible, assigning the same qubit to a different task once it is released. If the released qubits remain entangled with other parts of the system upon their release, allocating them as fresh qubits and using them in a different part of the computation can affect the results of the whole program—without the developer being any the wiser.

These kinds of bugs are really hard to track down, and the quantum hardware runtime cannot check whether a qubit is entangled with others when it is released! Running the program on a simulator that performs these kinds of checks can be very helpful in catching such bugs early.

Quantum software developers rely on the full state simulator to run their programs on small instances of problems, to verify that they produce the expected answer, and to develop unit tests. For example, the Quantum Katas (*https://oreil.ly/w19qn*)

rely on the full state simulator for verifying that the learners' solutions to the programming problems are correct.

The program visualization tools provided by the full state simulator are also extremely useful for learning. They allow a person at the start of their quantum computing journey to write and run lots of small programs to experiment with quantum computing, confirm their understanding of the basic principles, and find the gaps in their knowledge. We will learn more about the testing and debugging tools offered by the full state simulator in Chapter 8.

Resources Estimator

The *resources estimator* is another commonly used simulator from the QDK toolkit. It estimates the resources required to run a Q# program on a quantum computer, even if the program is too large to actually be executed, either on the full state simulator or on quantum hardware.

It is often important to get a good idea of the resources required by an algorithm beyond its asymptotic runtime and memory usage. As in classical computing, two algorithms for solving the same problem that have the same asymptotic complexity (*https://oreil.ly/HrczR*) can differ widely in the actual resources consumed in different scenarios. Besides, the exact implementation details of an algorithm, such as choosing a data structure used on one of the steps of the algorithm, can alter its complexity dramatically.

Example: Asymptotic Complexity of Sorting Algorithms

Consider, for example, the classical sorting task. There are multiple algorithms that sort an array of N numbers in O(N log N) operations in the average case. However, they differ in their memory usage, the number of operations required in the best or worst case, as well as in other properties. For example, in-place sorting algorithms will require a small, fixed amount

---

of memory outside the given array, while others might require O(log N) or even O(N). All these properties might define which algorithm is most suitable for a certain application, so it is important to evaluate them before making a decision.

Historically, the authors of papers presenting quantum algorithms and their implementations had manually calculated the estimates of the resources required to run them, and these estimates were hard to reproduce and to verify (not to mention to do accurately in the first place!). Given the limitations of the full state simulation that we've discussed earlier, and the small sizes of currently available quantum hardware, tools such as the resources estimator are often the only way to automatically evaluate a specific implementation of an algorithm.

Internally, the resources estimator doesn't actually simulate the program execution like the full state simulator does. Instead, it walks through the program, taking note of qubit allocation and release, and quantum gates and measurements, without performing any of these actions. The output of the resources estimator is a short list of the resources the program used during its execution. The two main parameters in the list are the number of qubits used by the program (the "width" of the corresponding circuit) and the time it would take to run (the "depth" of the circuit). Other statistics include the numbers of certain types of single-qubit gates, CNOTs, and measurements.

Trace Simulator

The *trace simulator* is similar to the resources estimator (and is, in fact, the foundation on which the latter is built) in that it doesn't simulate the program execution but only traces the steps of this execution. It can perform more finely tuned resources estimation, such as estimating the depth of the circuit with different "execution times" assigned to different gates. (The resources estimator uses the default settings, in which the most "time-consuming" gate is the T gate, and the rest of the gates are ignored, effectively giving a T-gate count.) The trace simulator can also run some program validations, checking that the program never tries to use a qubit allocation that is already released, or to call a multiqubit gate with the same qubit in several roles. If you're working with a small program that can be executed on a full state simulator, it will catch these bugs and throw an exception at runtime, but using the trace simulator is a good way to detect these kinds of issues in larger programs.

NOTE

Both the resources estimator and the trace simulator estimate the resources and perform program validations for only one execution path of the program. If a program has multiple possible execution paths, such as branches of an if-else statement, one run of the resources estimator will cover only one execution path. To estimate the resources required in the average scenario, you'll need to write a classical host program to run the resources estimator multiple times with different input parameters and aggregate the results.

Toffoli Simulator

The *Toffoli simulator* simulates program execution gate-by-gate, as long as the program uses a very limited set of gates: X, CNOT, and their controlled variants with multiple control qubits. These gates are sometimes called "classical," since a quantum system that starts in the $|0\rangle$ state and uses only those gates can never get to a superposition state, transitioning only between the basis states of the system, which correspond to classical integers.

Since this simulator doesn't need to represent the superposition states of the system, it can encode the states as an array of Boolean values, one per qubit. This makes the simulation very efficient and allows the simulator to run programs that use tens of thousands of qubits. However, it cannot simulate the programs that use the full power of quantum computation, since the program running on the Toffoli simulator has access only to the basis states of the system.

The Toffoli simulator turns out to be surprisingly useful for validating so-called *reversible computations*—quantum computations that implement classical functions, such as quantum oracles, quantum arithmetic, and so on.

Sparse Simulator

The *sparse simulator*, introduced in QDK 0.24, performs an accurate and complete simulation of your quantum program, the same as the full state simulator does. The difference between these two simulators is the representation of the state vector they use. The full state simulator stores the complete state vector, while the sparse simulator uses a sparse representation, storing just the nonzero elements of the state vector together with their indexes. This allows the sparse simulator to reduce the memory required to store the quantum state if it has few nonzero elements, and thus to simulate larger programs compared to the full state simulator.

The sparse simulator is useful for exploring algorithms that employ quantum states with few basis states in superposition.

Noise Simulator

The *noise simulator* simulates the program's behavior in the presence of noise, unlike the simulators you saw earlier, which simulate its behavior under perfect conditions. You can use this simulator to model noisy hardware devices—and currently, that means all of them!

The noise simulator represents the quantum state of the program as a density operator rather than as a state vector. It allows you to configure the noise model to use in the simulation with the help of the QuTiP library (*https://qutip.org*), associating certain types of noise with specific gates used in your Q# program. For example, you can specify that each time your program applies an X gate to a qubit, there is a small probability of that qubit's state being flipped again, or that each time your program applies a Z gate to a qubit, there is a small probability of that qubit being reset to the $|0\rangle$ state.

Running Q# Programs

Now that we've covered the tools we can use to run Q# programs locally on your computer, let's discuss different ways to do that.

The rest of this chapter will show you how to run a simple Q# program that simulates a series of biased coin flips. It takes two numbers—an integer n and a floating-point number pTrue—as an input and returns an array of n Boolean values. Each of the return values will represent the result of a single flip of a biased coin, being true with the probability pTrue, and false with the probability 1 - pTrue.

Example 6-1 shows the basic Q# code that implements this example. Note that it uses two operations—the main operation FlipBiasedCoinN and the helper operation FlipBiasedCoinOnce that simulates a single coin flip by preparing a qubit in an uneven superposition and measuring it.

Example 6-1. Biased coin flip program in Q#

```
namespace BiasedCoins {
    open Microsoft.Quantum.Arrays;
    open Microsoft.Quantum.Intrinsic;
    open Microsoft.Quantum.Math;

    /// # Summary
    /// Generates a single random bit that represents
    /// an outcome of a biased coin flip.
    /// # Input
    /// ## pTrue
    /// The probability to generate true.
    operation FlipBiasedCoinOnce(
        pTrue : Double
```

```
    ) : Bool {
        use q = Qubit();
        // Prepare state (1-pTrue)|0⟩ + pTrue|1⟩.
        Ry(2.0 * ArcSin(Sqrt(pTrue)), q);
        // Measure the state to get the result.
        return M(q) == One;
    }

    /// # Summary
    /// Generates a series of random bits that
    /// represent outcomes of a biased coin flip.
    /// # Input
    /// ## n
    /// The number of bits to generate.
    /// ## pTrue
    /// The probability to generate true.
    operation FlipBiasedCoinN(
        n : Int, pTrue : Double
    ) : Bool[] {
        // Use library operation to repeat operation
        // several times and accumulate the results.
        return DrawMany(FlipBiasedCoinOnce, n, pTrue);
    }
}
```

This example is not particularly exciting on its own, but it has all the key features I'll need to discuss the ways to run Q# code and the way it needs to be modified in each scenario. In particular, it takes several parameters of different types, and it returns a nontrivial value.

Let's see how to run this program using different methods.

Standalone Q#

The simplest way to run Q# code is *standalone Q#* mode.

In this mode, the project consists of:

- Q# code in one or several *.qs* files
- The *.csproj* file, which defines the project type, the version of the QDK to use, and other project settings

This minimalistic setup can be very convenient for quick prototyping and developing small projects or unit tests that don't require heavy classical computations. However, it is not the most elegant way to implement an end-to-end hybrid quantum-classical application, since it does not allow you to integrate Q# code with classical code easily.

Setting up the project

A standalone Q# project is defined using a *.csproj* project file based on the MSBuild format, similar to .NET projects (*https://oreil.ly/hVzAZ*). Example 6-2 shows a typical example of a *.csproj* file defining a standalone Q# project.

Example 6-2. Project file for a standalone Q# project

```
<Project Sdk="Microsoft.Quantum.Sdk/0.24.201332">
  <PropertyGroup>
    <OutputType>Exe</OutputType>
    <TargetFramework>net6.0</TargetFramework>
  </PropertyGroup>
</Project>
```

Let's take a closer look at the key properties defined in this file.

Project

The Sdk attribute set to Microsoft.Quantum.Sdk indicates that the project is a Q# project and should be built using the specified version of the Microsoft QDK.

OutputType

This specifies the project type: Exe indicates an executable, and omitting this property indicates a library or a unit test project.

TargetFramework

This specifies the target framework for the project: it should be net6.0 for Q# projects created with QDK 0.24 or later, or netcoreapp3.1 for projects created with earlier QDK versions.

The rest of the properties follow the standard MSBuild format (*https://oreil.ly/webds*).

If you need to use Q# code from other projects or NuGet packages in your project, you can use project references or package references, respectively, the same as you would in a classical .NET project. For example, to add a reference to the NuGet package Microsoft.Quantum.Xunit (a library for testing Q# programs using the xUnit framework), add the following snippet to your *.csproj* file under the Project tag:

```
<ItemGroup>
  <PackageReference
    Include="Microsoft.Quantum.Xunit"
    Version="0.24.201332" />
</ItemGroup>
```

Writing the quantum code

In this mode, one of the operations in the Q# code has to be annotated with @EntryPoint attribute. This will let the compiler know which of the operations should be the *entry point*—the operation called first when the compiled program is executed. Each Q# project can have at most one @EntryPoint attribute:

```
@EntryPoint()
operation FlipBiasedCoinN(
    n : Int, pTrue : Double
) : Bool[] {
    return DrawMany(FlipBiasedCoinOnce, n, pTrue);
}
```

If the project contains unit tests, each of the unit test operations has to be annotated with @Test attribute. We will discuss writing unit tests in Q# in more detail in Chapter 8.

Running the program

You can run standalone Q# projects in the same way you run classical .NET projects. Let's start with considering the case of the entry point operation taking no parameters.

If you're using the command line, type **dotnet run** to build and run your project. (You can first use **dotnet build** to build the project without running it.)

If you're using Visual Studio, you can set your Q# project as the startup project, and press Ctrl+F5 (Start without debugging) or use the green Start button on the Visual Studio toolbar to run the program.

These commands will build your project and run it using the full state simulator. The return value of the entry point operation, as well as any debug information printed by the Q# code, will be printed to the standard output of the program.

If you want to choose a different simulator to run your program on, you can do so via the command-line parameters. Use the option **--simulator** (or the shorthand **-s**), followed by the name of the simulator to use.

Table 6-1 lists the values you can pass to the --simulator command to run your program on different simulators.

Table 6-1. Command-line arguments that invoke different simulators

Argument	Simulator
No argument or `QuantumSimulator`	Full state simulator
`ResourcesEstimator`	Resources estimator
`ToffoliSimulator`	Toffoli simulator
`SparseSimulator`	Sparse simulator

For example, to run your program on the sparse simulator, use the following command:

```
dotnet run -s SparseSimulator
```

The `dotnet run` command also accepts a variety of options that are common for classical .NET projects and not specific to Q# code.

If you're using Visual Studio to run your Q# projects, you can configure the command-line parameters to pass to your code as follows: right-click on your project, choose Properties > Debug and fill the command-line parameters in the Application Arguments field.

Passing parameters to the quantum code

Recall that the entry point operation in our coin-flip example takes two parameters—an integer and a floating-point number:

```
operation FlipBiasedCoinN(
    n : Int, pTrue : Double
) : Bool[]
```

This means that you need to pass these parameters to the operation when running the project; otherwise, you'll get an `Option ... is required` error for each missing parameter.

You can pass the parameters to the Q# code from the command line as well. To do this, use command-line options with names that match the names of the parameters. Names defined in camel case are converted to kebab-case style names, called with two dashes as a prefix; the rest of the names are used with a single dash.

In our example, the parameters n and pTrue will be converted to command-line options n and p-true:

```
dotnet run -n 10 --p-true 0.3
```

Table 6-2 shows how you can pass parameters of different data types to a Q# project.

Table 6-2. Passing parameters to a standalone Q# project via the command line

Data type	Example	Notes
Int	--n-dec 10 --n-hex 0xAE	Can use decimal and hexadecimal literals.
BigInt	-n 9223372036854775808	No L postfix, unlike in Q# BigInt literals.
Double	--p-true 0.3	Can omit decimal point for integer values, unlike in Q# Double literals.
Bool	-b1 true -b2 FALSE	Values are case insensitive.
String	-s1 Hi -s2 "Hello World"	Can omit double quotes for strings without spaces.
Result	-r1 0 -r2 One	Values are case insensitive; 0 and 1 values can be used instead of Zero and One.
Pauli	-basis PauliX	Values are case insensitive.
Range	-r1 1..3 -r2 9..-1..0	Does not support spaces inside range values.
Array	-a 1 2 3	Space-separated list of array elements.

Passing qubits, tuples, user-defined types, or callables to the entry point operation is not supported.

Q# with a Classical Host

As discussed earlier, combining Q# code with a classical host program, wherein the Q# code is called as a subroutine by the host, is the most generic way to implement a quantum application. It combines the strengths of existing classical libraries and tools with the computational speedup offered by quantum computing.

Currently, Q# supports two kinds of classical host programs, .NET languages and Python. While the logic of integrating Q# with any language is similar, the project setup and the syntactic details differ depending on the language, so I will discuss these languages separately.

In both cases, the Q# code itself remains the same as in Example 6-1. You only need to modify the Q# code compared to the example in the standalone Q# or in Q# Jupyter Notebooks cases. The classical host program will use the Q# code as a library that provides quantum computing functionality.

In both cases you will run the hybrid application the way you normally run applications using that language, such as from the command line or from a Python Jupyter Notebook.

Q# with .NET Host

We will start with .NET languages, which include C#, Visual C++, F#, and Visual Basic.NET. For simplicity I will give the code samples in C#; the rest of the languages will use a similar approach, adjusted for each language's syntax. You can find the equivalent examples for other .NET languages in the supplemental materials repository (*https://oreil.ly/xHUmz*).

NOTE

You can follow the installation instructions (*https://oreil.ly/ cKJZz*) to set up the QDK for Q# with .NET host, and the project creation instructions (*https://oreil.ly/TCHec*) to create a Q# library project with .NET host.

Setting up the project

To run Q# code from a .NET application, you need to define it as a library using a *.csproj* file. The contents of the file will differ slightly from the standalone Q# project we looked at in Example 6-2. Example 6-3 shows a typical example of a *.csproj* file defining a Q# library.

Example 6-3. Project file for a Q# library

```
<Project Sdk="Microsoft.Quantum.Sdk/0.24.201332">
  <PropertyGroup>
    <TargetFramework>net6.0</TargetFramework>
  </PropertyGroup>
</Project>
```

Omitting the OutputType property indicates that this project is a library rather than an executable.

Distributing Q# Libraries as NuGet Packages

In this example I discuss using Q# libraries as project dependencies, which is the most convenient method for developing quantum and classical code for the same application together. If you are looking to distribute your quantum code as a library to other Q# users, similar to the QDK libraries, you'll want to release it as a *NuGet package*—a package for the .NET ecosystem that contains compiled code and related files and is distributed via the NuGet package manager.

In this case you'll need to modify your project properties to build a NuGet package from it, following the general NuGet package creation guidelines (*https://oreil.ly/g4cSt*). Your users will then add your package to their quantum or classical projects as a package dependency.

Once you've defined a Q# library, either as a project or as a NuGet package, you can use it as a dependency in your regular .NET application. Example 6-4 shows a typical example of a *.csproj* file defining a C# application with a dependency on a quantum library.

Example 6-4. Project file for a C# application using a Q# library

```
<Project Sdk="Microsoft.NET.Sdk">
  <PropertyGroup>
    <OutputType>Exe</OutputType>
    <TargetFramework>net6.0</TargetFramework>
  </PropertyGroup>

  <ItemGroup>
    <ProjectReference Include=
    "..\quantum-library\BiasedCoinsLibrary.csproj" />
  </ItemGroup>
</Project>
```

Notice that the C# project uses Microsoft.NET.Sdk as the SDK, the same as purely classical C# projects. Using Microsoft.Quantum.Sdk is necessary only for Q# projects.

With this project dependency, you can call any noninternal operations and functions defined in your quantum code.

Calling Q# code from C#

Calling a Q# operation from C# host program requires two steps.

First, *create an instance of a simulator* from the Microsoft. Quantum.Simulation.Simulators namespace that you'll use to run your code. You can use a using directive for that namespace in order to avoid writing out the fully qualified name of the simulator.

Table 6-3 lists the simulator classes available and the simulators they represent.

Table 6-3. C# classes that represent different simulators

Class	Simulator
QuantumSimulator	Full state simulator
ResourcesEstimator	Resources estimator
QCTraceSimulator	Trace simulator
ToffoliSimulator	Toffoli simulator
SparseSimulator	Sparse simulator

Creating an instance of the Toffoli simulator will look as follows:

```
using Microsoft.Quantum.Simulation.Simulators;
...
var toffoli = new ToffoliSimulator();
```

Note that the full state simulator, implemented by the Quantum Simulator class, implements the IDisposable (*https://oreil.ly/ PhHAx*) interface. This means that you need to call the Dispose method for the simulator instance after you're done with it. The easiest way to do this is to rely on the C# using statement (*https://oreil.ly/0nFg7*):

```
using var fullStateSim = new QuantumSimulator();
```

Second, *call the Run method of the Q# operation* you want to call. This method is automatically generated for all Q# callables. The first argument of this method is the simulator instance you want to use. The rest of the arguments match the parameters of the Q# operation you're calling.

The Run method generated for the Q# operation is asynchronous (*https://oreil.ly/z6G6h*), reflecting the fact that program execution on quantum hardware can potentially run for a long time. This means that you need to use either the await operator (*https://oreil.ly/SH6fu*) or the .Result property to wait until the method execution completes and to get its result:

```
var bits = FlipBiasedCoinN
              .Run(fullStateSim, 10, 0.3).Result;
```

Passing parameters to the quantum code

The arguments accepted by the Q# operation called from the C# code are converted into parameters of the Run method, starting with the second parameter. The return value of the Q# operation is converted into the return value of the Run method of the corresponding C# data type. Table 6-4 shows how different Q# data types map onto C#.

Table 6-4. Representation of Q# data types in C# host

Q# data type	C# data type	Notes
Int	long	
BigInt	System.Numerics. BigInteger	
Double	double	
Bool	bool	
String	string	
Result	Microsoft. Quantum.Simulation. Core.Result	Enum: Result.Zero and Result.One
Pauli	Microsoft. Quantum.Simulation. Core.Pauli	Enum: Pauli.PauliI, Pauli.PauliX, Pauli. PauliY, and Pauli.PauliZ
Range	Microsoft. Quantum.Simulation. Core.QRange	Class: constructor takes either two parameters (start and stop) or three parameters (start, step, and stop)
Array	Microsoft. Quantum.Simulation. Core.QArray	Class: constructor takes a C# array literal of a matching type, for example, new QArray<long>(new long[]{1, 2, 3});
Tuple	tuple	

You cannot pass qubits, user-defined types, or callables to a Q# operation called from a .NET host.

Q# with Python Host

Now let's take a look at how to do all these things with Python as the classical host program.

Setting up the project

To run Q# code from a Python program, place the *.qs* files in the same folder as the *.py* file(s) defining the host program. You can use a supplementary *.csproj* file to define any dependencies used by Q# code, but this is not required to set up interaction with the Python host.

Calling Q# code from Python

Calling a Q# operation from a Python host program requires three steps.

First, *import qsharp module* to enable Q# interoperability—using Q# operations in the Python program. After this, the namespaces defined in Q# code will be available to Python code as new modules, allowing you to *import the operations and functions* you intend to use:

```
import qsharp
from BiasedCoins import FlipBiasedCoinN
```

Once you've imported the Q# operation, it behaves as a Python class that implements a certain set of methods. To run this operation, *call a method of the Q# operation* that runs it on one of the available simulators. Table 6-5 lists the methods available and the simulators they invoke. All the simulator instances are created with their default parameters; you cannot customize simulator parameters from the Python host.

Table 6-5. Python methods for running the operation on different simulators

Method	Simulator
`.simulate()`	Full state simulator
`.estimate_resources()`	Resources estimator
`.toffoli_simulate()`	Toffoli simulator
`.simulate_sparse()`	Sparse simulator
`.simulate_noise()`	Noise simulator

Running an operation on the full state simulator will look as follows:

```
bits = FlipBiasedCoinN.simulate(n=10, pTrue=0.3)
```

Passing parameters to the quantum code

The arguments accepted by the Q# operation called from the Python code are converted into parameters of the corresponding methods of the Python version of this operation. Note that the arguments of the Q# operation become keyword-only arguments of the Python methods, with keywords matching the names of the arguments in Q#. The return value of the Q# operation is converted into the return value of the corresponding method.

Table 6-6 shows how different Q# data types map onto Python.

Table 6-6. Representation of Q# data types in Python host

Q# data type	Python data type	Notes
Int	int	
BigInt	int	
Double	float	
Bool	bool	
String	str	
Result	int	Does not support `Zero`/`One` literals.

Q# data type	Python data type	Notes
Pauli	int	Integers 0, 1, 2, and 3 represent PauliI, PauliX, PauliZ, and PauliY, respectively.
Array	list	
Tuple	tuple	

You cannot pass ranges, qubits, user-defined types, or callables to the Q# operation called from a Python host.

Q# Jupyter Notebooks

Q# Jupyter Notebooks are a web-based interactive environment for working with Q#. They allow you to define and import Q# code, run it on simulators, and visualize it using tools that are not available in other Q# environments (we'll discuss them in Chapter 8). They also provide standard Jupyter Notebooks functionality, such as creating documentation cells with rich text and math formulas using Markdown and LaTeX, and inserting media such as images and videos.

Q# Jupyter Notebooks offer a convenient setup for quick prototyping and experimenting with small code snippets. Because they allow you to combine interactive code with text and media, they are perfect for creating tutorials, interactive learning tools, demos, and presentations. For example, the Quantum Katas use Q# Jupyter Notebooks extensively to offer tutorials that combine theoretical material, interactive exercises, and solution explanations.

NOTE

You can follow the installation instructions (*https://oreil.ly/cKJZz*) to set up the QDK for Q# Jupyter Notebooks.

Setting up the notebook

A Q# Jupyter Notebook can exist on its own, without an underlying Q# project. The only file required is the *.ipynb* file that defines the notebook itself.

You can also use the notebook as a "frontend" for the "backend" Q# code defined in *.qs* files existing in the same folder. In this case the IQ# kernel will compile those files upon its startup and make their contents available to the notebook cells.

If you need to use Q# code from another project or package in your code cells, you can use %project (*https://oreil.ly/fU7Uq*) or %package (*https://oreil.ly/vq5aw*) magic commands. Both commands will load the references on the fly, when the cell is executed.

Alternatively, you can define a *.csproj* file on the Q# "backend" used with the Q# Jupyter Notebook "frontend," add package and project references you need to it, and add <IQSharp LoadAutomatically>true</IQSharpLoadAutomatically> to the <PropertyGroup> tag. In this case, the IQ# kernel will load the references upon its startup. This approach works great when combined with Q# "backend" files in the same project, allowing you to do all the project setup work in the background and only bring to the notebook the portions of Q# code and magic commands that you want to demonstrate.

Writing the quantum code

Q# code written in Jupyter Notebooks doesn't need to be wrapped in a namespace declaration. Q# Jupyter Notebooks define a working namespace automatically, and all Q# code written in the notebook cells is compiled as part of that namespace.

You can open namespaces in the code cells in the same way as in the other modes of Q# code. Two namespaces, Microsoft.Quantum.Intrinsic and Microsoft.Quantum.Canon, are open by default, so you don't need to reopen them in your code. You also don't need to reopen namespaces in each cell; it is sufficient to open a namespace once in one of the cells, and it will remain available to the cells executed later.

The notebooks don't support annotations such as @EntryPoint or @Test to define the operations that should be executed. Instead, you need to call the operations you want to execute explicitly.

Running the program

Both code compilation and code execution in Jupyter Notebooks are done via *cell execution*.

Once you've written some Q# code in a notebook cell, execute this cell using Ctrl+Enter (⌘+Enter on macOS). This will compile the code and output the compilation errors, if any. If the code compiles successfully, the cell execution will output a list of operations, functions, and user-defined types defined in this cell that are now available to the cells executed later.

To run the code, you need to use a *magic command*—one of the special commands that control Jupyter Notebooks—followed by the name of the operation you want to run.

Figure 6-3 shows Example 6-1 executed in the Q# Jupyter Notebooks environment.

```
open Microsoft.Quantum.Arrays;
open Microsoft.Quantum.Math;

operation FlipBiasedCoinOnce(pTrue : Double) : Bool {
    use q = Qubit();
    Ry(2.0 * ArcSin(Sqrt(pTrue)), q);
    return M(q) == One;
}

operation FlipBiasedCoinN(n : Int, pTrue : Double) : Bool[] {
    return DrawMany(FlipBiasedCoinOnce, n, pTrue);
}
```

  • FlipBiasedCoinOnce
  • FlipBiasedCoinN

```
%simulate FlipBiasedCoinN n=3 pTrue=0.3
```

  • False
  • False
  • True

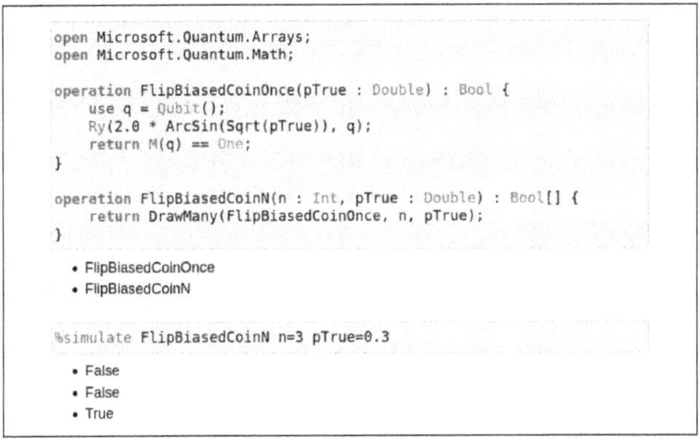

Figure 6-3. Running Q# in the Jupyter Notebooks environment

Table 6-7 lists the most commonly used magic commands that run the Q# operations on various simulators. All the simulator instances are created with their default parameters.

Table 6-7. Magic commands for running the operations on different simulators

Command	Simulator
`%simulate`	Full state simulator
`%estimate`	Resources estimator
`%toffoli`	Toffoli simulator
`%simulate_sparse`	Sparse simulator
`%experimental.simulate_noise`	Noise simulator

You can find a complete list of IQ# magic commands in the documentation (*https://oreil.ly/NR6E0*). I will return to them in Chapter 8 when I discuss the program visualization tools offered by Q# Jupyter Notebooks.

Passing parameters to the quantum code

To pass the parameters to the operation simulated using one of the magic commands, you will use `parameter=value` pairs. The parameter names are spelled in the same way as in the Q# code. In our biased coins example, running the operation with the right parameters on the full state simulator looks as follows:

```
%simulate FlipBiasedCoinN n=10 pTrue=0.3
```

Table 6-8 shows how you can pass parameters of different data types to an operation in Q# Jupyter Notebooks.

Table 6-8. Passing parameters to a Q# operation in Jupyter Notebooks

Data type	Example	Notes
`Int`	`n=10`	Can use only decimal literals.
`BigInt`	`n=9223372036854775808`	No L postfix, unlike in Q# `BigInt` literals.

Data type	Example	Notes
Double	pTrue=0.3	Can omit decimal point for integer values, unlike in Q# Double literals.
Bool	b1=true b2=FALSE	Values are case insensitive.
String	s1=Hi s2="Hello World"	Can omit double quotes for strings without spaces.
Result	r1=0 r2=1	Does not support Zero/One literals.
Pauli	basis=PauliX	Values are case insensitive; integers 0, 1, 2, and 3 can be used instead of PauiI, PauliX, PauliZ, and PauliY, respectively.

Q# Jupyter Notebooks do not support passing qubits, ranges, tuples, arrays, user-defined types, or callables to the operation called via a magic command. If you need to pass more complicated parameters to the operation, consider defining a parameterless wrapper operation that defines those parameters and passes them to your original operation.

Conclusion

In this chapter, you've learned a lot about the quantum software development process and about the tools available to you to run Q# programs.

In the next chapter, we will return to discussing the development of Q# programs. You will learn about the Q# libraries included in the QDK and about using them to write high-level Q# code.

CHAPTER 7

Microsoft Quantum Development Kit Libraries

This chapter offers an overview of the Q# libraries shipped as part of the Microsoft Quantum Development Kit. These libraries include everything you need to write Q# programs, from the quantum gates and measurements built into the language to commonly used patterns and tools that help you write complicated high-level algorithms. I've mentioned several library functions and user-defined types in the previous chapters, but I've never talked about them in a systematic way; in this chapter, I'll amend that.

The Q# libraries can be clustered in two groups: the standard libraries that provide shared functionality used in a lot of Q# code, and the domain-specific libraries that target solving very specialized problems in domains such as chemistry and machine learning.

This chapter starts with a quick overview of how you can get the standard and the advanced libraries, find information about them, and use them in your code.

After that, I review the functionality offered by the standard libraries, calling out some of the more frequently used operations and functions and providing examples. You can find more detailed code examples of using each library covered in this chapter in the supplemental materials repository (*https:// oreil.ly/kATle*).

Getting and Using the Libraries

The Q# libraries are distributed as NuGet packages via the NuGet package manager (*https://www.nuget.org*), similar to the libraries for .NET languages. The libraries are organized in namespaces, each including operations, functions, and user-defined types focused on a certain topic. (One exception to this rule is the `Microsoft.Quantum.Canon` namespace, which is a "catchall" of sorts: it hosts a broad variety of operations and functions that don't have a more specialized namespace defined for them.)

You can find the details on all functionality offered by the Q# libraries in the API documentation (*https://oreil.ly/GvpHK*). Each page covers one operation, function, or user-defined type and describes its purpose, its signature, inputs and outputs of the callables, and usage examples. Each page also includes the NuGet package that provides access to that particular callable or UDT, and the namespace that needs to be opened to use it.

Libraries' namespaces are independent of NuGet packages that deliver these libraries. Callables that reside in the same namespace can come from different packages, and one package can define multiple namespaces. The only restriction is that the names of callables and user-defined types within the same namespace have to remain unique.

For example, the callables that are in the `Microsoft.Quantum. Arithmetic` namespace in Q# libraries come from two separate NuGet packages, Microsoft.Quantum.Standard and Microsoft.Quantum.Numerics, and the operations offered by the Microsoft.Quantum.Standard NuGet package are organized into multiple namespaces according to their purpose.

To use certain library functionality in your Q# code, you need to make sure that the NuGet package that provides it is included in your project. Here is where to look:

- The standard libraries are distributed as part of the Microsoft.Quantum.Standard NuGet package that is included in all Q# projects by default via the Microsoft.Quantum.Sdk package, so you can use it immediately after you've created a Q# project.

- A small subset of built-in language tools, such as attributes used to mark entry points, unit tests, and deprecated functionality, is distributed as the Microsoft.Quantum.QSharp.Foundation NuGet package that is also included in the Microsoft.Quantum.Sdk package.

- The domain-specific libraries are distributed as separate NuGet packages that need to be included in the *.csproj* file as package references (see Table 7-3). Once you add the references to the corresponding packages to the project file, the Q# compiler will fetch the packages during the next project build.

Here is an example of a *.csproj* file that defines a Q# project that has access to both the standard libraries and the domain-specific machine learning library:

```
<Project Sdk="Microsoft.Quantum.Sdk/0.24.201332">
  ...
  <ItemGroup>
    <PackageReference
        Include="Microsoft.Quantum.MachineLearning"
        Version="0.24.201332" />
    ...
  </ItemGroup>
  ...
</Project>
```

Once you've included the right NuGet packages in your project, you can access individual callables and UDTs either by opening the namespaces that define them at the beginning of the Q# file or by using their fully qualified names, as I've shown in Chapter 1. Namespace `Microsoft.Quantum.Core` is open by default in all Q# files.

Standard Libraries

Now that you know how to use the libraries in your Q# code, let's take a look at the standard libraries available and the functionality they provide. I'll start with the "classical" libraries—libraries that provide nonquantum functionality—and then move on to strictly quantum libraries, starting with `Microsoft.Quantum.Intrinsic`.

Microsoft.Quantum.Core: Built-In Functions and Attributes

The `Microsoft.Quantum.Core` namespace offers several functions and attributes that are defined as "built-in" for Q#. This means the namespace is open by default and can be accessed without opening the namespace explicitly.

Built-in functions

This namespace includes very few functions that are core to the language. The most common is the function `Length`, which returns the number of elements in the array. It also includes the type-parameterized `Default`, which returns the default value of the type parameter, and the functions that return individual parameters of the input `Range`; however, these are much less frequently found in Q# code.

Attributes

Q# attributes are implemented as user-defined types, but their syntax is quite different. One of the most commonly used attributes is `@EntryPoint`, used to mark the operation called first during the program execution in standalone Q# mode, as you saw in Chapter 6. The `@Deprecated` attribute marks operations and functions as *deprecated*—obsolete and best avoided. It can be used with a single `String` parameter that provides the name of the callable or the UDT to be used instead of the deprecated one. This attribute is very useful for library developers, who may need to either rename the callables or fundamentally change the way they work when they change the libraries' public interfaces. You'll see another popular attribute, @Test, in Chapter 8 when I discuss writing Q# unit tests.

Microsoft.Quantum.Convert: Data Type Conversions

As you've seen in Chapter 2, Q# is a strongly typed language that prohibits implicit type conversions. This means that any time you need to use an expression of one type in a context that requires a value of a different type, you need a way to perform an explicit type cast. For example, the addition operator in Q# expects operands of matching types, so if you need to add values of types Int and Double, you must explicitly convert the first operand to the Double type.

The Microsoft.Quantum.Convert namespace is a collection of type conversion functions that act on a variety of primitive data types and arrays. Such functions follow a similar naming convention: a function that converts TypeA to TypeB will be called TypeAAsTypeB. It will take a single input of type TypeA and produce an output of type TypeB that has an equivalent value to the input value.

In the example of adding values of types Int and Double, you can convert Int to Double using the IntAsDouble function:

```
open Microsoft.Quantum.Convert;

function MixedSum(a : Int, b : Double) : Double {
    return IntAsDouble(a) + b;
}
```

Most of the functions in this namespace belong to two main groups:

Functions that convert between two primitive types
These include conversions between Int, BigInt, and Double, as well as between Bool and Result, and also

conversions of these types to String. Note that Q# doesn't offer string parsing, that is, this library doesn't offer conversions from String to other types.

Functions that convert between primitive types and arrays of other types

Most of these functions convert between integer types and arrays of Bool that represent little-endian notation of these integers.

The parameterized function FunctionAsOperation is worth a separate note: it converts a function of type 'Input -> 'Output to an operation of type 'Input => 'Output that calls this function and returns its return value (recall that the names of type parameters used in definitions of parameterized functions have to start with a tick; see Chapter 5). This function can be useful when you want to use a callable that takes an operation as input and pass it a function as an argument, since, as you've seen in Chapter 5, you cannot pass a function directly if the callable signature requires an operation. Instead, you need to use this function to perform an explicit cast.

Some of the libraries that I'll discuss later that define additional data types define matching type conversion functions as well. For example, the Microsoft.Quantum.Arithmetic namespace defines type conversion functions BigEndianAsLittle Endian and LittleEndianAsBigEndian; similarly, the Microsoft. Quantum.Math namespace defines functions ComplexAsComplex Polar and ComplexPolarAsComplex.

Microsoft.Quantum.Logical: Logical and Comparison Functions

The Microsoft.Quantum.Logical namespace is a collection of functions that implement equality and inequality operators, comparison operators, and logical operators, as well as the conditional expression.

Most of the functions in this namespace reimplement the built-in operators you've seen in Chapter 3. For example:

- Logical functions And, Or, and Not implement corresponding logical operators.
- Equality, inequality, and comparison functions implement corresponding comparison operators.

The latter functions follow the standard naming convention: a function that compares values of a certain type will be named based on the comparison it performs (Equal, NotEqual, Less Than, LessThanOrEqual, and so on), with a suffix that indicates the type it acts on (EqualI, LessThanD, and so on).

You'll see the suffixes denoting the type of callable inputs quite often in the Q# libraries. Table 7-1 provides a list of suffixes for the most common types you'll see.

Table 7-1. Type suffixes in Q# library functions

Type	Suffix
Int	I
BigInt	L
Double	D
Bool	B
String	S
Result	R
Microsoft.Quantum.Math.Complex	C
Microsoft.Quantum.Math.ComplexPolar	CP
Microsoft.Quantum.Arithmetic.LittleEndian	LE
Microsoft.Quantum.Arithmetic.BigEndian	BE
Microsoft.Quantum.Arithmetic.FixedPoint	FxP

You should not treat the functions that implement built-in operators as the default way to use the corresponding operators. If you just need to compare two values in your code or construct a logical expression, operators are a more concise and readable way to do that. Instead, these functions are designed for use with type-parameterized callables. As you've seen in Chapter 5, you have to pass any operators the type-parameterized callable uses to process its inputs as additional inputs. The functions from this namespace make sure you don't have to reimplement the wrappers for the standard logical operators yourself.

Additionally, the `Microsoft.Quantum.Logical` namespace offers several logical functions that do not have matching built-in operators:

- Equality and inequality functions compare library types `Complex` and `ComplexPolar` from the `Microsoft.Quantum.Math` namespace, which I'll discuss later.

- Approximate equality and inequality comparison functions `NearlyEqualD` and `NotNearlyEqualD` check whether the floating point arguments are within 1E-12 from each other. They are often more useful than the exact comparison operators due to floating point imprecision.

- A type-parameterized function known as `Lexographic Comparison` returns a function that performs lexographic comparison of two arrays based on a provided element comparison function. Array `a1` is said to be *lexographically earlier* than array `a2` if array `a1` is a prefix of the array `a2` or if, in the first position where their matching elements differ, the element of the array `a1` is less than the element of the array `a2`.

`LexographicComparison` is a great example of a function used together with the comparison functions from this namespace. Here, for example, is how you define and use a function to compare arrays of integers using only library functions:

```
open Microsoft.Quantum.Logical;

let lessThanAI =
    LexographicComparison(LessThanOrEqualI);
```

```
let a1 = [1, 2, 3];
let a2 = [1, 2, 4];
Message($"{lessThanAI(a1, a2))}");
```

Microsoft.Quantum.Bitwise: Bitwise Functions

The `Microsoft.Quantum.Bitwise` namespace is a collection of functions that implement bitwise operators. Similar to `Microsoft.Quantum.Logical`, most of the functions in this namespace reimplement the built-in operators you've seen in Chapter 3 for use with other functions: And, Or, Not, Xor, Left Shifted*, and RightShifted*.

Note that in this namespace the functions And, Or, and Not perform bitwise manipulation of integer inputs, as opposed to logical manipulation of Boolean inputs performed by the functions with the same names from the `Microsoft.Quantum.Logical` namespace. If you need to use functions with the same names from different namespaces in the same Q# file, you'll need to use their fully qualified names to disambiguate them.

Microsoft.Quantum.Math: Classical Math and Arithmetic

The `Microsoft.Quantum.Math` namespace is a collection of functions that implement various arithmetic operators and mathematical functions for classical inputs:

Functions that implement arithmetic operators
> Similar to the previous two namespaces, the functions Plus, Minus, Times, DividedBy, Negation, Pow, and Modulus implement built-in arithmetic operators you've seen in Chapter 3 for different data types.

Functions that offer access to classical mathematical functions
> Such functions are typical for math libraries of other programming languages, such as the System.Math namespace in C#. Examples include minimum and maximum functions, trigonometric functions, factorial, greatest common divisor, and others.

Types and functions that work with rational and complex numbers

This namespace defines the user-defined types `Fraction`, `Complex`, and `ComplexPolar`, which represent rational and complex numbers, and basic functions for working with these types.

Microsoft.Quantum.Random: Random Numbers and Probability Distributions

The `Microsoft.Quantum.Random` namespace offers operations, functions, and user-defined types that define and work with probability distributions.

The most frequently used tools from this namespace are the operations that generate random numbers or draw random samples from a given probability distribution:

- `DrawRandomInt` and `DrawRandomDouble` draw from discrete and continuous uniform distributions, respectively.

- `DrawRandomBool` returns `true` with the given probability `successProbability` and `false` with probability `1 - successProbability`.

- A generalization of that, `DrawCategorical` takes an array of floating-point numbers and returns a random index within that array. The probability of each index being drawn is proportional to the corresponding array element, divided by the sum of all elements.

These functions use the same pseudorandom number generators that classical programming languages use.

Note that all callables that produce any sort of randomness have to be defined as operations rather than functions. As you've seen in Chapter 5, Q# functions represent deterministic computations, and drawing random numbers is anything but that!

Microsoft.Quantum.Arrays: Generic Array Manipulation

The `Microsoft.Quantum.Arrays` namespace is a collection of array manipulation routines.

Unlike the namespaces I've discussed earlier in this chapter, most operations and functions in this namespace are type-parameterized, acting on arrays of parameterized (variable) type rather than arrays of fixed type. This makes them convenient in a broad range of scenarios, whenever you're working with arrays.

Table 7-2 provides a list of the most commonly used operations and functions in the `Microsoft.Quantum.Arrays` namespace, grouped by their purpose.

Table 7-2. `Microsoft.Quantum.Arrays` namespace

Name	Summary
Array comparison	
EqualA	Generic function that checks two arrays for equality, given a function that checks equality of array elements
Array elements access and reshaping functions	
Head/Tail	Returns the first/last element of the array
ElementAt	Returns the element of the array at the given index; `ElementAt(ind, a)` returns `a[ind]`
Rest/Most	Returns all elements of the array except for the first/last one
Subarray	Returns array elements at the given indexes
Excluding	Returns all array elements except the ones at the given indexes
Reversed	Returns a reversed array
Sorted	Returns a sorted array, using the given comparison function for sorting

Name	Summary
Flattened	Given an array of arrays, returns a concatenation of its elements
Chunks/ Partitioned	Splits an array into several subarrays of equal (Chunks) or varying (Partitioned) lengths
Windows	Returns all subarrays of the input array of the given length

Search and condition checks functions

Name	Summary
All/Any	Returns true if all/any elements of the array satisfy the given predicate
IndexOf	Returns the index of the earliest array element that satisfies the given predicate, or −1 if no such element is found
Where	Returns indexes of all array elements that satisfy the given predicate
Filtered	Returns array elements that satisfy the given predicate
Count	Returns the number of array elements that satisfy the given predicate

Combining several arrays

Name	Summary
Zipped/ Zipped3/ Zipped4	Returns an array of tuples of 2/3/4 elements, in which each tuple contains corresponding elements from all input arrays
Interleaved	Returns an array constructed of the elements of the first array at indexes 0, 2, …, and the elements of the second array at indexes 1, 3, …

Array transformations

Name	Summary
ForEach/Mapped	Returns an array that consists of results of applying the given operation/function to each element of the input array
Enumerated	Returns a tuple array that combines the elements of the input array with their indexes in that array

Name	Summary
Fold	Reduces an array by successively applying a binary function, that is, computes a value f(...f(f(initial State, array[0]), array[1]), ...)

Microsoft.Quantum.Intrinsic: Basic Quantum Gates and Measurements

The `Microsoft.Quantum.Intrinsic` namespace offers operations that implement the standard quantum gates and measurements.

Standard quantum gates

These operations implement the standard set of single- and multiqubit quantum gates used to express quantum algorithms. The single-qubit gates include the Pauli gates I, X, Y, and Z, the phase gates S and T, the Hadamard gate H, and a variety of rotation gates. The multiqubit gates include the CNOT, CCNOT, and SWAP gates. Note that the gates defined in this namespace are by no means an exhaustive list of quantum gates you can use in Q# programs! Rather, they are the most common building blocks used by other library operations, and you can use them to define your own gates as well.

Standard measurements

The operation M implements one of the most common measurements, a single-qubit measurement in computational basis. The operation Measure implements a more generic measurement—joint multiqubit measurement defined by an array of Pauli bases. Additionally, this namespace defines the operations Reset and ResetAll. These reset a single qubit or an array of qubits to the $|0\rangle$ state by measuring them and possibly applying an X gate after the measurement to adjust the state of the qubits. You can find a variety of other measurement operations in the `Microsoft.Quantum.Measurements` namespace, which I'll discuss shortly.

Logging function

> You can use the logging function `Message` to print a message, typically to the console output or the Jupyter Notebook output cell.

Microsoft.Quantum.Diagnostics: Testing and Troubleshooting Quantum Programs

The `Microsoft.Quantum.Diagnostics` namespace includes the following tools for inspecting various elements of quantum programs and verifying their correctness:

Program inspection tools

> The tools in this group allow you to inspect elements of quantum programs. `DumpMachine` and `DumpRegister` functions print information about the current state of all qubits allocated by the program and of the given set of qubits, respectively. The `DumpOperation` operation prints the information about the given operation, such as the matrix of the quantum gate it implements.

Classical condition checks (facts)

> Each function in this group tests a classical condition and throws an exception if the condition is not met. The universal function `Fact` fails if its Boolean argument is false, similar to `Assert.IsFalse` in C# or `assert` in Python. Its counterpart `Contradiction` fails if its Boolean argument is true. The rest of the functions match the equality and near-equality checks on values of different types from the `Microsoft.Quantum.Logical` namespace, failing if the values are not equal, similar to `Assert.AreEqual` in C# or `assertEqual` in Python.

Quantum condition checks (assertions)

> Each operation in this group tests a quantum condition and throws an exception if the condition is not met. These operations rely on nonphysical capabilities of quantum simulators, such as the ability to access the state of the system directly without measuring it, so they will typically

have no effect if the program is running on quantum hardware. The most commonly used assertions are `Assert AllZero`, which checks that each of the given qubits is in the $|0\rangle$ state, and `AssertOperationsEqualReferenced`, which checks that the two given operations implement the same quantum transformation.

Attributes for defining tests

This namespace defines several attributes used when defining Q# unit tests. The most common of these is `@Test`, used to mark operations as xUnit unit tests and make them discoverable by unit testing tools such as Visual Studio Test Explorer.

I'll return to this namespace in Chapter 8 when I talk about testing and debugging tools and techniques in more detail.

Microsoft.Quantum.Measurement: Additional Measurement Routines

The `Microsoft.Quantum.Measurement` namespace provides operations that implement various kinds of measurements beyond those included in the `Microsoft.Quantum.Intrinsic` namespace:

- `MResetX`, `MResetY`, and `MResetZ` are single-qubit variants of `Measure`, performing a single-qubit measurement in the corresponding Pauli basis and resetting the qubit to the $|0\rangle$ state afterward.

- `MeasureAllZ` is a multiqubit variant of `Measure` in which all the Pauli bases are Pauli Z; in other words, `MeasureAllZ` measures the parity of the qubit array and returns a single `Result` value.

- `MultiM` performs a single-qubit measurement in the computational basis M for each of the qubits in the array and returns an array of measurement results.

Some of the other namespaces offer extra measurement operations on top of the ones in this namespace. For example, `Microsoft.Quantum.Arithmetic` namespace includes the operations `MeasureInteger` and `MeasureFxP`, which measure each of the qubits in an array and convert the measurement results into an integer or a double, respectively.

Microsoft.Quantum.Preparation: Quantum State Preparation

The `Microsoft.Quantum.Preparation` namespace offers routines that prepare various quantum states. Some of the operations in this namespace are relatively advanced; here are several of the simpler and the more useful ones:

- `PrepareUniformSuperposition` prepares a uniform superposition of the first N basis states from $|0\rangle$ to $|N{-}1\rangle$, inclusive.

- `PrepareArbitraryStateD` and `PrepareArbitraryStateCP` prepare an arbitrary superposition state, described by the given array of real or complex amplitudes, respectively.

- Both operations `ApproximatelyPrepareArbitraryStateD` and `ApproximatelyPrepareArbitraryStateCP` act similarly to the previous two operations; however, instead of preparing the described state exactly, they prepare some state that is close enough to the described one.

All operations in this namespace implement state preparation routines as sequences of simpler gates and thus can be used in programs that run on a quantum device. (Recall that Q# doesn't allow you to set the quantum state of the program directly, as I've described in Chapter 2.)

Microsoft.Quantum.Arithmetic: Quantum Arithmetic

The `Microsoft.Quantum.Arithmetic` namespace defines types that represent integers and fixed-point numbers as qubit arrays, as well as operations for working with them. These tools allow Q# programs to perform arithmetic computations on superpositions of integers, which is an essential part of most quantum algorithms:

Data types

The key user-defined types in this namespace are `Little Endian` and `BigEndian`, which represent integers in the little-endian and big-endian system, respectively, and `FixedPoint`, which represents a fixed-point number.

Arithmetic and comparison operations

Most operations in this namespace implement arithmetic and comparison operators for these UDTs. Some arithmetic operations have several implementations in this namespace that differ in complexity. For example, all three of the operations `RippleCarryAdderD`, `RippleCarry AdderCDKM`, and `RippleCarryAdderTTK` add two integers represented as `LittleEndian` in place, but they use different numbers of auxiliary qubits and various types of gates, leading to different circuit width and depth for each operation. Choosing the right implementation for your goals can impact the efficiency of your code, so make sure to read the API documentation carefully.

Measurements

You can use operations `MeasureInteger` and `MeasureFxP` to measure the `LittleEndian` and `FixedPoint` variables and convert measurement results into integers and floating-point numbers, respectively.

Asserts

This namespace defines several additional assertions that act on the UDTs from this namespace rather than on raw qubit arrays. For example, `AssertProbInt` checks that the probability of measuring a specific basis state when measuring a `LittleEndian` variable has the expected value.

Microsoft.Quantum.Canon: Catchall

The `Microsoft.Quantum.Canon` namespace is a "catchall" namespace that hosts a variety of useful but harder to classify operations and functions. It is one of the larger namespaces, so if you are looking for some functionality that doesn't belong to any of the more specialized libraries, check whether this namespace offers it.

Here are several examples of useful routines you can find in this namespace:

Controlling operations
> The two functions from this namespace that I use most frequently are `ControlledOnInt` and `ControlledOn BitString`. These functions produce a controlled variant of the given operation, similar to the `Controlled` functor, but they allow more flexibility in the condition under which the operation is applied. `ControlledOnBitString` applies the operation on the target qubits if the control qubits are in the basis state described by the given bit string (for the `Controlled` functor, this bit string is always 1...1). `ControlledOnInt` applies the operation on the target qubits if the control qubits are in the basis state described by the given integer in little-endian format (for the `Controlled` functor, this integer is always 2^N-1, where N is the number of control qubits).

Special gates
> This namespace includes several gates. `CX`, `CY`, and `CZ` are shorthand for controlled specializations of the corresponding Pauli gates with a single control qubit. `Apply DiagonalUnitary` applies relative phases to the basis states of a qubit array.

Applying callables to arrays

ApplyTo is a group of operations that typically apply the given operation to some elements of an array. For example, the ApplyToEach operation applies an operation that acts on a certain type to each element of an array of that type; ApplyToElement applies an operation to a certain element of an array; ApplyToMost applies an operation to each array element except the last one; and so on. A lot of these operations combine an operation application with matching functions from the Microsoft.Quantum.Arrays namespace.

Composing callables

The function Bound produces an operation that applies each of the given operations in turn. Similarly, Compose combines functions, producing a function that is equivalent to evaluating the two given functions in turn.

Quantum Fourier transform

Quantum Fourier transform is one of the key tools of quantum computing. The QFT and QFTLE operations apply quantum Fourier transform to a quantum register in BigEndian and LittleEndian formats, respectively. ApproximateQFT applies the approximate variant of the transform that discards the smallest rotations to get a more efficient transformation that is close enough to the full QFT.

Miscellaneous utility operations

Some utility operations can be emulated easily using regular Q# syntax and are useful in very specific situations— for example, if you like to write your code in a functional style rather than an imperative one. Fst and Snd allow you to get the first and second elements of a two-element tuple, respectively, without using full tuple deconstruction. Ignore and NoOp allow you to ignore any value, typically a return value from a callable; they are a type-parameterized function and operation, respectively, that take an arbitrary value as an input and return Unit. Delay allows you to delay a callable execution: you provide the callable and its arguments via partial application, and call the result later with an extra `Unit` parameter to execute the callable. `Repeat` is an equivalent of a `for` loop, repeating an operation a certain number of times.

The operations in this namespace that take operations as arguments often come in several variants, depending on the specializations the operation argument has. For example, `ApplyToEach` can be used with any operation, but the result does not have a controlled or an adjoint specialization; `ApplyToEachA` can only be used with operations that have adjoint specialization, and the resulting operation has an adjoint specialization; `ApplyToEachCA` requires that the operation argument has both controlled and adjoint specializations, and has both specializations in turn. If you're using such operations in code that needs to have certain specializations defined, you need to choose the right variant of the operation.

Advanced Libraries

As of early 2022, Q# has several domain-specific libraries. Additionally, some of the standard libraries provide rather advanced functionality. I will not discuss these libraries in further detail in this book, since using them requires significant knowledge of specialized areas of quantum computing.

Table 7-3 provides a list of domain-specific and advanced standard libraries.

Table 7-3. Advanced Q# libraries

Namespace(s) Microsoft.Quantum.*	NuGet package(s) Microsoft.Quantum.*	Purpose
AmplitudeAmplification	Standard	Amplitude amplification tools
Arithmetic	Standard Numerics	Numerics library: advanced integer and fixed-point arithmetic functionality for quantum numbers
Characterization	Standard	Tools for learning properties of quantum states and processes, including tomography and phase estimation
Chemistry Chemistry.JordanWigner Chemistry.Jordan Wigner.VQE Research.Chemistry	Chemistry Research.Chemistry	Quantum chemistry library: tools for working with classical computational chemistry packages and implementing quantum chemistry solutions
ErrorCorrection	Standard	Quantum error correction

Namespace(s) Microsoft.Quantum.*	NuGet package(s) Microsoft.Quantum.*	Purpose
MachineLearning MachineLearning.Datasets	MachineLearning	Machine learning library: tools for implementing and using circuit-centric classifiers, and example datasets
Oracles	Standard	Functions and UDTs to convert quantum operations to oracles in the formats used by other libraries
Simulation	Standard	Coherent simulation of dynamics of quantum systems
Synthesis	Standard	Implementing quantum operations based on various classical descriptions, such as permutations and Boolean functions. Includes the operation ApplyUnitary that implements a gate described by a given unitary matrix.

Once you're ready for a deep dive, you can read more about these libraries in the QDK documentation (*https://oreil.ly/8dXZ6*).

Conclusion

In this chapter, you've learned enough about the QDK standard libraries to start using them to write your Q# programs.

In the next chapter, I'll discuss testing and troubleshooting Q# programs using the tools provided by the QDK.

CHAPTER 8

Testing and Debugging

This chapter describes the visualization, testing, and debugging tools and techniques available to you as a Q# developer. As with previous chapters, some of these tools will be similar to their equivalents in classical software development; the others will be unique to quantum software development, reflecting the fundamental differences between the two.

The first part of this chapter covers the tools used for inspecting elements of Q# programs, both classical and quantum. In it, I show:

- How to print the quantum state of your program during its execution
- How to inspect the matrix of the transformation implemented by a quantum operation
- How to observe the quantum circuit that represents the structure of the program
- How to follow the program state through its execution

The second part of this chapter covers the tools used to test quantum programs. I'll start by showing two ways to write tests for quantum programs: using standalone Q# programs or combining them with classical host code. After that, I'll dig deeper into the library functions and operations used for unit testing quantum programs, and the various scenarios in which they can be useful.

The tools and techniques I describe in this chapter rely on running quantum code on the simulators you saw in Chapter 6. These tools take advantage of direct access to the quantum state of the program as it is executed and allow you to test the programs without using quantum devices, which makes testing very accessible for quantum software developers. None of these tools are designed to be used when running quantum code on quantum devices.

Inspecting Elements of Q# Programs

Q# offers a variety of tools for inspecting Q# programs; let's see what they are, starting with the more familiar "classical" ones, and then moving on to the tools unique to quantum computing.

Classical Variables

The techniques for inspecting classical variables used in quantum programs are very similar to the debugging techniques available for classical programming languages. They include printing the values of the variables at different points of program execution and observing the variables "live."

The `Message` function from the `Microsoft.Quantum.Intrinsic` namespace, available in all Q# environments, is used to print classical variables. Depending on the way you run your Q# code, it will print its string argument to the console output (for standalone Q# or Q# with a classical host) or to the Jupyter Notebook output cell.

You can use `Message` to print any values, but for some of the Q# types, the output will be of limited use. For example, `Message` will print the values of arrays, tuples, and UDTs, but for the callables it will print their names rather than their full signatures, and for the qubits it will print their internal IDs rather than their states.

Additionally, if you use Visual Studio or Visual Studio Code for Q# development, you can use some of this IDE's debugging capabilities. In Visual Studio, for example, the Q# extension supports setting breakpoints and stepping through the code to get to the fragment of interest, as well as inspecting the values of classical variables.

Quantum States

Software developers are used to monitoring the values of all variables during a classical program's execution and even changing them on the fly to see how that affects the program's behavior. It is natural to look for a similar ability to directly inspect and modify the quantum state of the Q# program.

However, Q# is designed to run programs on quantum devices, and thus it reflects the limitations imposed by quantum physics. From the physics point of view, when you have a quantum system in some state, you cannot get complete information about its state from a single observation; you can only extract a bit or several bits of information by performing a measurement. Furthermore, the act of measurement changes the state of the system to match the measurement results, so it is not a practical debugging tool.

To help you debug your quantum programs while taking into account the physics limitations, Q# offers several functions that work only on quantum simulators. Since quantum simulators are themselves classical programs, they allow full access to their internal state during program simulation and thus can be used for reporting the quantum state.

The `DumpMachine` function from the `Microsoft.Quantum.Diagnostics` namespace prints the information about the current quantum state of the program, as tracked by the simulator on which it is running. The related function `DumpRegister` from the same namespace prints the information about the quantum state of the given subset of qubits, if possible. If it is not possible (for example, if these qubits are entangled with any others), DumpRegister prints a warning instead.

The output of this function depends on how the simulator represents the quantum state during the program execution. The most commonly used simulator, full state simulator, tracks quantum state as a vector of complex numbers that describe the amplitudes of the basis states of the system. For it, the DumpMachine output contains the list of the basis states and the amplitude, the measurement probability, and the relative phase for each of them. The basis states are denoted as integers in little-endian encoding, rather than the bit strings you'll often see used in Dirac notation to describe states with few qubits.

The following snippet shows the code to prepare and print the two-qubit superposition state $\frac{1}{3}(|00\rangle + 2i|01\rangle - 2|11\rangle)$ using the library operation PrepareArbitraryStateCP:

```
use qs = Qubit[2];
PrepareArbitraryStateCP([
        ComplexPolar(1., 0.),
        ComplexPolar(0., 0.),
        ComplexPolar(2., PI()/2.0),
        ComplexPolar(-2., 0.)
    ],
    LittleEndian(qs));
DumpMachine();
```

The output will look like Figure 8-1.

```
# wave function for qubits with ids (least to most significant): 0;1
|0):     0.333333 + -0.000000 i  ==     ***
|1):     0.000000 +  0.000000 i  ==
|2):    -0.000000 +  0.666667 i  ==     *********
|3):    -0.666667 +  0.000000 i  ==     *********
                                  [ 0.111111 ]    --- [ -0.00000 rad ]
                                  [ 0.000000 ]
                                  [ 0.444444 ]     ↑   [  1.57080 rad ]
                                  [ 0.444444 ] ---     [  3.14159 rad ]
```

Figure 8-1. DumpMachine output (text format)

When running Q# code in Q# Jupyter Notebooks, the output produced by `DumpMachine` and `DumpRegister` is more visually appealing and can be customized using the `%config` magic command. You can use this command to modify a lot of parameters, such as:

- The notation for the basis states (the default little-endian integers, big-endian integers, or bit strings)

- The columns included in the output (you can exclude the measurement probabilities and the relative phases from the output)

- The rows included in the output (you can choose to exclude basis states with amplitudes smaller than a certain threshold, which can be very convenient for examining sparse states on multiple qubits)

Figure 8-2 is an example of what the `DumpMachine` output can look like for the same superposition state $\frac{1}{3}(|00\rangle + 2i|01\rangle - 2|11\rangle)$ with some of these modifications applied.

```
%config dump.basisStateLabelingConvention="BitString"
%config dump.truncateSmallAmplitudes=true
%config dump.phaseDisplayStyle="none"
%simulate RunIt
```

Qubit IDs	0, 1	
Basis state (bitstring)	**Amplitude**	**Meas. Pr.**
$|00\rangle$	$0.3333 - 0.0000i$	11.1111%
$|01\rangle$	$-0.0000 + 0.6667i$	44.4444%
$|11\rangle$	$-0.6667 + 0.0000i$	44.4444%

Figure 8-2. `DumpMachine` output (Jupyter Notebook format)

Other simulators have their own formats for `DumpMachine` output. The Toffoli simulator tracks the state of the system as an array of individual qubit states, each of them 0 or 1, so the `DumpMachine` output will be just a bit string. Resources estimator and trace simulator don't support these functions at all, since they don't track the quantum state of the system during program execution, only the resources required to run it.

Note that the Dump functions always produce a text report of the program state rather than returning it as a value. There are two reasons for this design choice. First, it allows you to run code that uses these functions on multiple simulators without modifications, regardless of the format in which each simulator reports its internal state. Second, it ensures that your Q# programs cannot gain access to their quantum state to make any nonphysical decisions based on it, and thus can be executed on quantum hardware without changes. In this case the runtime will define the Dump functions either to print some kind of hardware diagnostic or to do nothing, without affecting the logic of the program.

Quantum Operations

Q# operations often implement quantum transformations of varying complexity, either specialized ones such as quantum oracles or general-purpose unitary transformations. It is convenient to be able to inspect the transformation implemented by an operation to make sure it matches your needs.

The `DumpOperation` operation from the `Microsoft.Quantum.Diagnostics` namespace prints the information about the transformation performed by the given operation. The operation passed as an argument to `DumpOperation` should act on an array of qubits. What about operations that act on an individual qubit, like most of the gates from the `Microsoft.Quantum.Intrinsic` namespace, or a combination of individual qubits and qubit arrays, like quantum oracles? To inspect such an operation, you have to define a wrapper operation for it that takes a single array argument, reshapes it into the right arguments, and calls that operation. After this, you'll use `Dump Operation` for that wrapper operation. If you need to inspect an operation that takes additional parameters of types other than qubit, you have to provide the values of those parameters using partial application (discussed in Chapter 5).

The following code snippet shows how to combine these approaches to print the matrix of the Controlled Rx gate, with the first qubit acting as the control and the second one as the target:

```
operation ControlledRxWrapper(
    qs : Qubit[],
    theta : Double
) : Unit is Adj + Ctl {
    Controlled Rx(Most(qs), (theta, Tail(qs)));
}

operation RunIt() : Unit {
    DumpOperation(2,
        ControlledRxWrapper(_, PI() / 2.0));
}
```

The DumpOperation output when running in Q# standalone mode looks as follows:

```
Real:
[[1, 0, 0, 0],
[0, 0.7071067811865476, 0, 0],
[0, 0, 1, 0],
[0, 0, 0, 0.7071067811865476]]
Imag:
[[0, 0, 0, 0],
[0, 0, 0, -0.7071067811865475],
[0, 0, 0, 0],
[0, -0.7071067811865475, 0, 0]]
```

Since, in general, quantum transformations are described using matrices of complex numbers, the DumpOperation output is split in two matrices: the first one shows the real components of the transformation matrix, and the second one shows the imaginary components.

When you run Q# code in Q# Jupyter Notebooks, the output produced by DumpOperation is more visually appealing, with the two matrices combined into a single matrix of complex numbers, as shown in Figure 8-3.

| Qubit IDs | | | 2, 3 |

$$\text{Unitary representation} \quad \begin{pmatrix} 1 & 0 & 0 & 0 \\ 0 & 0.707 & 0 & -0.707i \\ 0 & 0 & 1 & 0 \\ 0 & -0.707i & 0 & 0.707 \end{pmatrix}$$

Figure 8-3. `DumpOperation` output (Jupyter Notebook format)

Note that the matrix of the controlled Rx gate produced by `DumpOperation` differs from the one you might've seen in other quantum computing books and tutorials. Typically the matrix of a controlled Rx gate would have the identity matrix in the top right quadrant, the matrix of the Rx gate in the bottom left quadrant, and zeros in the other two quadrants.

This is explained by the fact that `DumpOperation`, like a lot of the Q# library operations, uses little-endian encoding for integers, including the indexes of the matrix elements. Thus, the second column of the matrix corresponds to the index 1 and the input state $|10\rangle$. The controlled Rx gate transforms it to the state $\frac{1}{\sqrt{2}}(|10\rangle - i|11\rangle)$, represented by the nonzero elements in the second and fourth rows of the matrix. The third column corresponds to the index 2 and the input state $|01\rangle$, unchanged by the controlled Rx gate, represented by the nonzero element in the third row.

In contrast, other quantum computing resources often use big-endian encoding for representing integers, in which the second column corresponds to the input state $|01\rangle$ and the third one to $|10\rangle$. You can modify the definition of `ControlledRxWrapper` in the example to use the second qubit as the control and the first one as the target:

```
operation ControlledRxWrapperBE(
    qs : Qubit[],
    theta : Double
) : Unit is Adj + Ctl {
    Controlled Rx(Rest(qs), (theta, Head(qs)));
}
```

This will have the effect of switching the operation from little endian to big endian, and DumpOperation will produce a more familiar matrix, shown in Figure 8-4.

Qubit IDs			2, 3
Unitary representation	$\begin{pmatrix} 1 & 0 & 0 & 0 \\ 0 & 1 & 0 & 0 \\ 0 & 0 & 0.707 & -0.707i \\ 0 & 0 & -0.707i & 0.707 \end{pmatrix}$		

Figure 8-4. DumpOperation output (Jupyter Notebook format, big endian)

Program Structure and Its Evolution

Q# Jupyter Notebooks offer additional tools for inspecting the structure of the program as a whole and for following the evolution of the quantum state of the program throughout its execution. These tools rely on program representation as a *quantum circuit*—a sequence of quantum gates and measurements applied to qubits.

Quantum circuits are a common way to visualize simple quantum programs or their building blocks, even though they are not powerful enough to express an arbitrary quantum computation. Common elements of quantum programs such as loops, classical conditional statements, and evolution of classical variables don't have conventional representation in terms of quantum circuits. At the same time, circuits can be a convenient way to get an idea of the quantum operations your program applies during its execution or to compare your program with another one.

The %trace magic command simulates a Q# program while tracking the gates and measurements applied during its execution, and then plots an interactive circuit that shows the program execution. By default the circuit shows only top-level operations. You can investigate their structure by clicking on each block to display the operations it comprises, all the way down to the intrinsic gates and measurements (Figure 8-5).

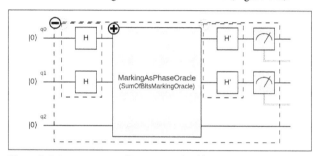

Figure 8-5. %trace output (Jupyter Notebook)

This command shows only the operations and gates executed in one run of the program, rather than the general program structure. For example, the last step of the quantum teleportation protocol applies different gates to finalize the teleported state depending on the outcomes of the measurements on the previous step. If you trace execution of this program, you'll see different circuits for different program runs.

Finally, the %debug magic command combines the effects of %trace and DumpMachine: it traces the program execution as a circuit that evolves gate by gate, while showing the changing quantum state of the program at the same time. This command can be very useful when observing the evolution of smaller programs, but the number of the evolution steps can quickly become overwhelming as the number of qubits and gates involved grows.

Testing Q# Programs

As with classical software, testing quantum programs is an important part of the quantum software engineering process. At the same time, new challenges arise from the fundamental differences between quantum and classical software. The QDK allows you to create unit tests for your Q# programs integrated with familiar frameworks and tools such as xUnit and Visual Studio Test Explorer, and it provides a variety of library tools that help you test different types of quantum program functionality.

Two Ways to Write a Test

There are two main ways that you can write a test for a Q# program.

First, you can combine the Q# code with the classical host program the way I showed in Chapter 6. The classical code will call the Q# code and verify the correctness of its results using the .NET or Python frameworks you normally use to implement and run unit tests. In this scenario you don't need to modify the Q# code in any way, since all the testing logic is hosted in the classical code.

Second, you can create standalone Q# unit tests, similar to standalone Q# projects, that perform all correctness checks within Q# code. The remainder of this chapter focuses on Q#-only unit tests and the library tools you can use to write them.

The techniques used for writing standalone Q# unit tests could in principle be used within the Q# Jupyter Notebooks environment, but Jupyter Notebooks are more commonly used for visualizations and interactive applications than for libraries and unit test development. A better approach is to extract the code that needs to be tested from the Q# notebook into a separate Q# project, use the Q# notebook as the frontend for this project, and create a standalone Q# test project that uses this project as a dependency.

Choosing Your Approach to Testing Q# Programs

Your choice of testing approach depends on your needs.

If you're looking to test a small code fragment in great detail and need low-level access to the program state—for example, to check that your quantum oracle implements the given classical function correctly or that your code prepares the right quantum state—standalone Q# unit tests are a better option. Most of the unit tests that cover Q# libraries are implemented as standalone Q# unit tests.

On the other hand, if you're looking to test an end-to-end scenario, such as modeling a property of a molecule or solving a puzzle using Grover's search, and you want to verify the end result rather than the individual program components, a combination of classical host code with Q# code can be a better approach.

One special case in which you definitely need the classical host code is testing Q# code that you expect to throw an exception. Since Q# doesn't offer exception handling, any exceptions thrown in the Q# code can be caught and confirmed only in the classical host code.

Standalone Q# Test Projects

Similar to standalone Q# projects, a standalone Q# test project consists of Q# code in one or several *.qs* files, and the *.csproj* file that defines the project properties. Example 8-1 shows a typical example of a *.csproj* file defining a standalone Q# test project.

Example 8-1. Project file for a standalone Q# test project

```
<Project Sdk="Microsoft.Quantum.Sdk/0.24.201332">
  <PropertyGroup>
    <TargetFramework>net6.0</TargetFramework>
    <IsPackable>false</IsPackable>
  </PropertyGroup>

  <ItemGroup>
    <PackageReference
      Include="Microsoft.Quantum.Xunit"
      Version="0.24.201332" />
    <PackageReference
      Include="Microsoft.NET.Test.Sdk"
      Version="16.4.0" />
    <PackageReference
      Include="xunit" Version="2.4.1" />
    <PackageReference
      Include="xunit.runner.visualstudio"
      Version="2.4.1" />
    <DotNetCliToolReference
      Include="dotnet-xunit" Version="2.3.1" />
  </ItemGroup>
</Project>
```

If you compare this example with Example 6-2, you'll notice several differences. The project properties do not include the OutputType property, and they indicate that the project is not packable; that is, it does not produce a NuGet package. Besides, the package references include a list of NuGet packages that enable unit testing functionality for Q# code (Microsoft.Quantum.Xunit and Microsoft.NET.Test.Sdk) and integration with various test runners for the xUnit framework (dotnet-xunit and xunit.runner.visualstudio). You can include additional project or package references, the same as you would for standalone Q# projects.

The Q# operations that implement unit tests have to be annotated with the @Test attribute defined in the Microsoft.Quantum.Diagnostics namespace. This lets the unit testing framework know which operations should be treated as unit tests.

Example 8-2 shows a simple unit test that verifies that the Q# function Squared evaluates the classical function f(x) = x² correctly.

Example 8-2. Defining standalone Q# unit tests

```
@Test("QuantumSimulator")
function TestSquared() : Unit {
    for i in -10 .. 10 {
        let expected = i * i;
        let actual = Squared(i);
        if actual != expected {
            fail "Incorrect return for input {i}: " +
                "expected {expected}, got {actual}");
        }
    }
}
```

The @Test attribute takes one string parameter that specifies the *execution target* of the test—the simulator to be used for running the test. You can use the .NET names of the built-in simulators ("QuantumSimulator", "ToffoliSimulator", and "SparseSimulator") as the execution targets. Alternatively, if you implement your own simulator or use a custom simulator, such as the CounterSimulator used by the Quantum Katas project, you can use the fully qualified name of that simulator as the execution target, for example, "Microsoft. Quantum.Katas.CounterSimulator". A test operation can have multiple @Test annotations with different execution targets if it can be executed on different simulators.

Example 8-2 tested purely classical functionality, so it didn't matter which simulator was used as the argument of the @Test attribute. Later in this chapter, I'll show you examples of tests that have to be executed on a specific simulator.

The operations annotated with @Test will show up as unit tests, one test for each @Test attribute, in viewers such as Visual Studio Test Explorer, where you can run them as you would normally.

If you work with the QDK from the command line, dotnet test will build the test project and run all the tests, reporting their status.

Testing Classical Conditions

The techniques for testing classical conditions used in Q# unit tests are extremely similar to those available for classical programming languages.

The Microsoft.Quantum.Diagnostics namespace offers a variety of functions that test a classical condition and throw an exception if the condition is not met; if the condition is met, the program execution continues normally. All Q# functions that test classical conditions are called *facts*, to distinguish them from *assertions*—operations that test quantum conditions.

Fact is the main function of this group: it takes a Bool condition and an error message as arguments, and throws an exception with this message if the condition is false. The following snippets of code are equivalent:

```
Fact(condition, "Test failed");

if not condition {
    fail "Test failed";
}
```

Contradiction is the opposite of Fact: it throws an exception with the given message if the condition is true.

The other functions in this namespace that offer checks for various conditions enhance the basic Fact functionality. They combine the Fact function with the equality and near-equality checks on values of different types implemented by logical and comparison operators or by functions from the

`Microsoft.Quantum.Logical` namespace. For example, the function `EqualityFactI` takes two integer parameters and compares them, throwing an exception if they are different. You can implement it as follows:

```
function EqualityFactI(
    actual : Int,
    expected : Int,
    message : String
) : Unit {
    Fact(actual == expected, message);
}
```

The especially useful facts are the ones that implement the bulkier checks. For instance, `AllEqualityFactI` checks that two integer arrays are equal—that is, they have the same length and are equal element-wise.

Testing Conditions on the Quantum State

The tools offered by the QDK to test various conditions on the quantum states during program execution rely on quantum simulators. Thus, these tools can use the nonphysical capabilities of quantum simulators, accessing the quantum state directly and running the tests on its precise parameters, rather than trying to gather statistics about the quantum state across multiple program executions and deriving conclusions from that.

The `Microsoft.Quantum.Diagnostics` namespace offers a variety of assertions for checking different properties of the current quantum state of the program. I'll cover several of the most straightforward ones, since they're the ones you're most likely to use, and let you explore the more niche ones yourself.

`AssertQubitIsInStateWithinTolerance` allows you to implement an arbitrary state check for a single qubit, as long as it is not entangled with other qubits. It takes a pair of complex numbers that describe the single-qubit state and checks whether the current state of the given qubit matches that state within a certain tolerance, throwing an exception if it doesn't. In the following example, the assertion checks that the Ry gate prepares the state $0.8|0\rangle + 0.6|1\rangle$:

```
use q = Qubit();
Ry(2.0 * ArcTan2(0.6, 0.8), q);
AssertQubitIsInStateWithinTolerance(
    (Complex(.8, .0), Complex(.6, .0)), q, 1E-9);
```

For multiqubit states, things are a little more complicated, since Q# libraries do not offer a multiqubit equivalent of the single-qubit assertion for an arbitrary state. There are several assertions that test various aspects of the quantum state of the given qubits. For instance, AssertProbInt tests the probability of measuring a certain basis state when measuring a qubit array in the computational basis. AssertAllZero checks that each of the qubits in the given array is in the $|0\rangle$ state.

You can implement an assertion for an arbitrary multiqubit quantum state by combining the AssertAllZero assertion with another library operation, PrepareArbitraryStateCP from the Microsoft.Quantum.Preparation namespace.

Let's say you need to check whether the array of qubits is in a state $|s\rangle$, described by an array of the complex amplitudes of all the basis states. If it is, applying Adjoint Prepare ArbitraryStateCP with those amplitudes should bring the qubits to the $|0...0\rangle$ state, since you know that applying Prepare ArbitraryStateCP to the $|0...0\rangle$ state prepares the state $|s\rangle$. If it is not, applying Adjoint PrepareArbitraryStateCP will bring the qubits to some state other than $|0...0\rangle$. This means that you can use AssertAllZero to figure out whether the qubits were in the state $|s\rangle$ or not! Since you need to make sure that any assertions you create don't modify the program state if they succeed, you need to apply PrepareArbitraryStateCP afterward to return the qubits to their expected state (recall that the within-apply statement will take care of that implicitly):

```
operation AssertQubitsAreInState(
    coefficients : ComplexPolar[],
    qubits : Qubit[]
```

```
    ) : Unit is Adj + Ctl {
        within {
            Adjoint PrepareArbitraryStateCP(
                coefficients, LittleEndian(qubits));
        } apply {
            AssertAllZero(qubits);
        }
    }
```

Comparing the Unitaries Implemented by Operations

A task that frequently arises when testing quantum programs is comparing two operations to check that they implement the same unitary transformation. This can be useful, for example, when you develop a new, more efficient way to implement a certain unitary transformation and want to make sure it's equivalent to the less efficient but more straightforward implementation.

The `Microsoft.Quantum.Diagnostics` namespace offers two main assertions to test whether two operations implement the same N-qubit unitary (up to a global phase): `AssertOperationsEqualInPlace` and `AssertOperationsEqual Referenced`. Both assertions throw an exception if the given operations implement different unitaries. In the following example, the assertion will throw an exception for any value of the parameter other than multiples of 2π, correctly identifying that the Ry gate is equivalent to the identity gate only for those values:

```
let theta = 2.0 * PI();
AssertOperationsEqualReferenced(1,
    ApplyToHead(Ry(theta, _), _), NoOp);
```

The assertions have the same API, but they differ in the approach they use and the complexity of that approach. `Assert OperationsEqualInPlace` compares the effects of the unitaries on a set of 4^N quantum states using the tools described in the previous section. It uses N qubits and 4^N calls to each of the unitaries. `AssertOperationsEqualReferenced` instead applies both unitaries to one half of a 2N-qubit state, calling each unitary only once.

Deep Dive: AssertOperationsEqualReferenced

How does `AssertOperationsEqualReferenced` work? It replaces the comparison of two unitary transformations with a check of quantum state equality (this is called *Choi–Jamiołkowski isomorphism*). Let's see how it does that, using two single-qubit unitary transformations A and B as an example.

We'll start with the two-qubit state $\frac{1}{\sqrt{2}}$ ($|00\rangle + |11\rangle$), and apply the transformations A and $B^\dagger$ (adjoint B) to the second qubit:

- After the first transformation, the two-qubit state will be $\frac{1}{\sqrt{2}}$ ($|0\rangle \otimes A|0\rangle + |1\rangle \otimes A|1\rangle$), and it will carry the information about the effects of the transformation A on both basis states.

- After the second transformation, the state of the qubits will be $\frac{1}{\sqrt{2}}$ ($|0\rangle \otimes B^\dagger A|0\rangle + |1\rangle \otimes B^\dagger A|1\rangle$).

Now,

- If the unitaries A and B are the same, $B^\dagger A$ is just the identity transformation, and the qubits will return to their initial state $\frac{1}{\sqrt{2}}$ ($|00\rangle + |11\rangle$).

- If the unitaries A and B are different, though, $B^\dagger A$ will differ from the identity in its effect on at least one of the basis states, and possibly on both, so the end state of the qubits will be different from their initial state.

This means that we just need to check whether the state of the qubits after applying the two unitaries is $\frac{1}{\sqrt{2}}$ ($|00\rangle + |11\rangle$), and we can do that using the tools we've seen earlier in this chapter.

Both operation comparison assertions rely on the use of a full state quantum simulator, so any tests that rely on them have to use the `@Test("QuantumSimulator")` annotation. You can also use this when deciding which of the assertions to use. If your test compares small operations such that the full state simulator can handle 2N qubits, you can use `Assert OperationsEqualReferenced`, which is faster in the number of operation calls. Otherwise you have to use `AssertOperations EqualInPlace`, which is slower in terms of the number of operation calls but less demanding in the number of qubits.

Conclusion

This chapter wraps up the second part of the book, which discussed the basics of the tools offered by the QDK to develop, run, and troubleshoot Q# programs.

This concludes the introduction to Q# and the QDK offered in this book. Now you are ready to start experimenting with your own quantum programs and discovering the subtler nuances and more specialized tools of the QDK. Enjoy!

Index

About the Author

Mariia Mykhailova is a principal software engineer in the Quantum Systems group at Microsoft. She joined the team in 2017, just in time to participate in the development of the first version of the Microsoft Quantum Development Kit. These days she works in education and outreach, developing new learning tools for quantum computing and quantum programming, such as the Quantum Katas, and coming up with ways to make learning engaging and exciting. She is also a part-time lecturer at Northeastern University Seattle, where she teaches Introduction to Quantum Computing.

Colophon

The animal on the cover of *Q# Pocket Guide* is a resplendent quetzal (*Pharomachrus mocinno*), a small bird found in southern Mexico and Central America. Resplendent quetzals live in the tropical forest and often settle in high mountain ranges. These birds prefer to inhabit decaying trees, stumps, and occasionally old hollows already made by woodpeckers.

Resplendent quetzals can grow to lengths of approximately 14 to 15 inches from the bill to the base of the tail. They have brilliant green plumage on their upper bodies and crested feathers on their heads. Males have impressive three-foot-long tails and bright red breasts and bellies; females, although similar in color, are duller and have shorter tails and gray breasts and bellies. While these birds primarily eat fruit, they also scavenge for insects, frogs, and snails.

The cover illustration is by Karen Montgomery, based on a black-and-white engraving from *Meyers Kleines Lexicon*. The cover fonts are Gilroy Semibold and Guardian Sans. The text font is Adobe Minion Pro; the heading font is Adobe Myriad Condensed; and the code font is Dalton Maag's Ubuntu Mono.

Lightning Source UK Ltd.
Milton Keynes UK
UKHW021235170622
404579UK00005B/10